# Coping with the Loss of a Sibling:

## *I Miss You, Gary*

By Roberta Stack-Costantino

Copyright© 2011 Roberta Stack-Costantino
Cover art by Stephanie Sibits
First Edition. All rights reserved.

FOR INFORMATION CONTACT:
Roberta Stack-Costantino
lifeguidanceandsolutions@gmail.com
robertastackcostantino@gmail.com

---

No part of this book may be reproduced in whole or part, in any form or by any means, electronic or mechanical, including photocopying, recording, or by any information storage and retrieval system now known or hereafter invented, without written permission.

Library of Congress Control Number: 2010917725
ISBN 978-1-935268-79-6

www.halopublishing.com

Printed in the United States of America

I dedicate this book to my wonderful brother, Gary, for giving me the confidence that I can do anything I set my mind to. Your brotherly love, friendship and continued protection have made me into the strong person I am.

I also dedicate this book to my loving father, Martin, who passed away suddenly on November 6, 2009, during the final draft of this book. His wonderful insight into life and guidance allowed me to believe that I could and would do anything I wanted. I love you and miss you both dearly. I would not be the person I am if it were not for the both of you.

# *Contents*

**Part One: "I Miss You, Gary"**
"I Miss You, Gary" Introduction ................................................. 1
Chapter One: I Miss You, Gary ..................................................... 3
Chapter Two: Stages of Grief ......................................................... 15
Chapter Three: Coping ................................................................... 21
Chapter Four: Negative and Destructive Behaviors ................. 35
Chapter Five: Sibling Rivalry ......................................................... 39
Chapter Six: Faith and Spirituality .............................................. 43
Chapter Seven: What You Can Do! ............................................. 47
Chapter Eight: Stories of Hope and Inspiration ....................... 53
Chapter Nine: What Would Help You Heal? ............................ 77

**Part Two: "Moving On"**
"Moving On" Introduction ............................................................ 83
Chapter Ten: Moving On ............................................................... 85
Chapter Eleven: Where Are You Now? ....................................... 91
Chapter Twelve: Where Do You Want To Be? .......................... 99
Chapter Thirteen:
Stories of Hope and Inspiration About Moving On ............. 103

**Part Three: "Reflections"**
"Reflections" Introduction .......................................................... 111
Chapter Fourteen: Reflections .................................................... 113
Chapter Fifteen:
Reflections on Stories of Hope and Inspiration ..................... 117

In Closing ....................................................................................... 125
Acknowledgements ....................................................................... 127
Bibliography ................................................................................... 129
Workbook ....................................................................................... 131
About the Author ......................................................................... 163

## *Part One*
## *"I Miss You, Gary"*

### INTRODUCTION

First, let me say, to those of you reading this book that have lost a sibling, I understand and know what you are going through. I also know that if you have been unhappy for too long, it is time you start living your life. This is the first of a series of books on coping with the loss of a sibling. This book goes through my story, stages of grief and coping, sibling rivalry, destructive behaviors, things you can do to help heal and other's stories for inspiration. Each person's story shows how people handle the death of a sibling in different ways. Some were able to move on and live happy lives and some are still in the process of healing after a tough time.

This book is to help you see that others are going through similar situations as you, and you can move forward and live a happy life! The following books in the series will move you forward through the healing process and with moving on with your life.

I wrote this book because I lost my brother, Gary, the oldest of four children, in 1981. He was in a single car accident; thankfully, no one else was involved. He apparently fell asleep or had some type of blackout that knocked him out. This caused him to hit a telephone pole and a tree, which resulted in severe head injuries. He supposedly never knew what happened. I live with that hope.

When I needed support in 1981, there were few books written about dealing with the loss of a sibling. We still seem to be the forgotten ones. At this point in your life, you may not even realize you are having a difficult time dealing with your loss. You may even think you are okay and do not need help; however, after reading this, my hope is you will better understand your feelings and grief.

I am not a psychologist or psychiatrist. I am presently working towards my certification in Grief Counseling, however, I am someone who has lived through the experience and changed my life because of it. You can too! If you have been trying to cope with a loss of a sibling for years, and still are unable to cope with the fact they are gone, please seek professional counseling to move yourself beyond this point. There are many people out there dealing with this that are turning their lives around because of the experience and are doing wonderful things to help others. Many wonderful organizations started because of these people wanting to help others with their grieving and coping, and offer counseling services for little or no cost.

# CHAPTER ONE
# *I Miss You, Gary*

I lost my brother to a car accident. He hadn't been feeling well for a while. A heavy equipment operator, he was about 6'1" and weighed about 140 pounds. He was tall and thin, but very muscular. Gary was a workaholic and dedicated worker. He had problems with his back due to driving the heavy equipment, which pounded on his body. At one point, he told his co-worker, Stan, he was having some chest pain. Stan noticed Gary was holding his left arm funny and told him to stop working. Gary's response was his job came first and he would finish his day. Stan never got Gary to go to the doctor. Gary had been to a doctor several months earlier and wore a back brace for support, but this was not enough or something else was obviously going on. We did not find out about this until Stan came to see us a while after Gary's death.

My brother is the most amazing person anyone could ever have as a sibling. And, yes...I said "IS." I say, "IS" because I still feel his presence. His spirit is with me every day of my life! I don't feel as if he is gone. His body is gone, but his spirit definitely lives on. You have probably experienced circumstances when you feel as if they were there, maybe leading you in the right direction, or when you missed getting in an accident, or you think or do something just in the nick of time. Now, let me tell you a little about Gary.

Gary really wasn't a sports fanatic. He was what they used to call a "grease monkey." He loved working on cars, painting cars or trucks, making things, drawing up blueprints of homes he wanted to build. He had a vision of what he wanted and would do it.

Gary could do anything and everything. He would take a burnt old 1934 Ford and turn it into a beautiful car. He took a burnt mobile home and made it into a palace. He seemed to have a thing about picking out the burnt, useless item and totally making it into something unbelievable; like the ugly duckling turned into a beautiful swan. I don't know how he did it! He made boats, water skis, and best of all, a rocking chair for me for Christmas, just because I wanted one! What kind of big brother does that? My big brother. If I mentioned I wanted something, that Christmas or birthday, it was there. No matter how far he had to go to get it for me.

Gary liked to act tough and people would shy away from him. However, he was all talk and no action. He had to be one of the most sensitive, nicest guys around. He had a heart of gold. One day, he bought a Harley Davidson motorcycle and started driving it around the yard. Mr. "Tough Guy", I think, saw a squirrel and turned that bike so fast he slid, almost hurting himself. I can't remember exactly what he said, but it was something like, "I would have run over it, but I slid on the wet grass." Yeah, right. Gary was too gentle and kind to do that. He wouldn't hurt a fly. One of his co-workers' granddaughters even nicknamed him "Sunshine." I think she was only about five or six-years-old and adored him.

I enjoy remembering all the things Gary and I did together as I write this. Another thing Gray did was always ask if I needed something. If he ran to Forest City to buy wood or went to Sears for a new tool, he would ask me if I needed something and would buy me those chocolate star candies. He bought me my first pair of jean overalls and my first pair of work boots, just like his, but without the steel toe. He also bought me my own Cat hat ("Caterpillar") that I still have. He had one, so of course I needed one, too. It's amazing how he would cart me around with him. I am so thankful for all those times now.

Gary didn't date much, but when he met the love of his life, Diane, who had cystic fibrosis, I was devastated. I thought, "How dare you take my big brother away from me." Well, of course, I should have known better; she really was a sweetheart. If my sisters went out, and I was going to be by myself and he was going to be with Diane, he would come home early to stay with me. A couple times Diane came with him. I started to like Diane, too. Gary wanted to marry her, but she was only 19-years-old and dying. I remember when he got the bad news at work. Diane passed away at the hospital. The cystic fibrosis had taken over her lungs and she could not fight it any longer. When he found out, he was working on a Mac truck. If you have any idea what a Mac truck is, you know it is a big, tough truck. Well the Mac truck suffered a fist-sized hole in its hood. Gary never even broke his hand, just bruised it, but suffered from a broken heart. I remember nights when it sounded like he was crying in bed. You have to understand, Gary never cried, at least not until Diane died. I don't believe he was ever really himself after that. He dated, but never found another Diane. He did date a girl named Stephanie, who still stops over my parent's house occasionally. It's always good to see her. It brings back good memories because they did a lot of things together. They went to the Bahamas and Hawaii, so at least he was able to travel and see some of the world.

Gary lived and worked on his projects. He was going to sign the papers to buy our grandparent's farmhouse the day he died. On that day, I decided somehow, someway and someday I would buy the house and fix it up. Maybe not as beautiful as he would have, but I would do my best to carry on his dream. I even wrote him a note and put it in his pocket in his casket promising him I would finish his dream. That promise came true in July of 2008 and I am in the process of fixing up our grandparent's old farmhouse, although, I didn't just do this for him. I also wanted this house. It has character, and reminds me of him.

Gary was 28-years-old when he died. It happened Labor Day weekend. I had finished my first week of college and was coming home I was so excited to see him. On that dreadful night, my oldest sister, Jeanette, who is 3 years younger than Gary was, and her husband, Tim, were taking our parents and her in-laws out to dinner. I remember my brother saying, "Jeanette was probably telling them she was knocked up!" I really didn't think much about that at the time. Gary and I talked a little more about my first week at college and his week before he went out and my boyfriend at the time came over.

It is somewhat funny, but I really don't remember anything else that day, except my conversation with Gary. I don't even remember my other sister being home or her conversations with Gary. I just remember Gary and me. I never really thought about until now.

It was later in the evening when my parents came home from dinner with my sister and brother-in-law. Yes, they did indeed tell everyone they were going to have a baby. This was the first grandchild for both sides of the family and what excitement everyone felt that night. The first niece or nephew. I waited for Gary to come home so I could tell him he was right! He never came home.

We woke up to a phone call from the hospital emergency room. "Are you the parents of Gary Stack?" There has been an accident. The dreaded phone call no parent wants to hear. Of course, they don't tell you anything other than you need to come to the hospital.

Gary had gone out to listen to a band at the country bar the night of the accident. I believe he started home around 1:30 or 2:30 a.m., when the band was done playing. It was a rainy night, and he was almost home, when he hit a telephone pole and an evergreen tree. Gary sustained severe head injuries and was dead on the scene. Thank God he died. He would not have wanted to live the life he would have lived if he had not died!

The accident was right in front of a house, so people heard the crash and immediately called the police. After a while, the people who lived in the house found out where we lived and brought over the eyeglasses Gary was wearing that flew across their yard, as well as some other belongings of Gary's that I can't remember. I always thought it was nice of them. It always kind of made me upset we never got those back because you knew they must have been a mess or flew off. Luckily, they were intact. They just flew off him with the force of the impact. For some reason it made me feel better they found the glasses and they weren't all broken up. I'm not really sure why I had this feeling, I just did. I guess it made it seem as if the hit to his head wasn't as bad as I thought, even though he died from massive head injuries.

## I Miss You, Gary

I can still feel the cold chill running down my body and thinking, "Oh my God! He is dead. He hit a telephone pole by Mr. T's Pizza." That was a pizza shop about a mile or so from where he actually died. Of course, my parents rushed off to the hospital with dread. When I saw my parents' car come back into the drive, I tried to feel hope that he was in the backseat lying down. They would be bringing him in the house any minute now, any minute now…well, they did not come in with Gary. Instead, you could tell by the way they looked that Gary was never coming home again.

The autopsy showed he possibly had one beer, if that and he was unconscious before he hit the pole. Another thank God! They said it possibly could have been some type of seizure or blackout. The autopsy was not able to show which. We just know it caused the accident. I remember they said something about how he was out before he hit because his eyes weren't black.

I can't tell you what I felt at that moment. You know how it feels and it is indescribably horrible. No words can describe how you feel right then. My whole world fell apart. My brother was and is my hero, as is my father and grandfather. Gary ran heavy equipment and I always joked that I would do the same, to be just like him. That was my dream when I was younger. We were a team. He made me feel safe and secure. No one was going to hurt his "Peewee." That was his nickname for me because I was tiny. He even named his first boat "Peewee" after me! (Now we are on Peewee IV). How was I going to go on? I just sat in his room with his cowboy hat on, smelled his clothes and his hats, and cried while sitting on his bed for what seemed like hours and hours. I distinctly remember the smell. It was the smell of diesel fuel from his work. I went through his things; touching everything thinking the more I touched them, the closer I would be to him. Maybe he would come back. I thought all sorts of wild things like if I thought about him being there, he would be there. If I bargained with God, he would bring him back. There is a lot I don't remember. I was in a daze. It was just a terrible nightmare I was hoping to wake up out of and have Gary pulling me around the house by my socks, or knotting my socks together so I couldn't stand up. I hoped I would wake up to him poking me in the ribs or hitting me in the elbow with a fork. However, I never woke up from the nightmare. The nightmare was reality, an all-too-real, horrible nightmare that would never end. My parents had to give me sedatives to try to calm me down, but they didn't work. I lay in bed all night thinking about him and crying. How could God do this to me? How could God do this to my parents? Why would this happen? Why was it happening now? What in the world did we do or did Gary do to deserve this? He always did good and helped everyone and anyone. WHY?

The next morning, being a strong Catholic family, we went to church to pray for him. Pray for what? Pray to whom? To the God who took my brother away? No way in hell was I going to do that. I wanted my brother back and right now! I knew praying to the God that took him away sure in hell wasn't going to bring him back. Those feelings lasted for quite awhile, until I started mellowing out about God taking my brother away. I did go to church that morning, but only for my parents. They did not need to deal with me or my issues with God at that moment. This was something I just had to do for them.

It took a while getting over blaming God. I started realizing that if this was going to happen, it was going to happen. Gary was meant to go at the time he did. I firmly believe this. I also found comfort in the realization he was where I think he wanted to be, with Diane. He was at peace. It took me some time to get to this point, but I did. I had to find peace, so I looked at all sides of the situation. I knew I couldn't continue blaming myself for having my boyfriend over and Gary leaving that night. I knew I had to find peace. I knew Gary would never want me to live like this. I had to find the peace and learn to cope with the new life I was dealt to live with, without my brother…my best friend.

The day after Gary died, after we got back from church, I was over at my grandparent's house, the one that was supposed to be his that very day. I started picking up beer tabs and cigar butts lying on the ground around the house because he had tossed them off as he worked on the siding. I know it's strange, but when you are distraught and in shock, you will take anything that is/was theirs. That is exactly what I was doing. I did eventually throw them out.

I walked next door to my house as one of our neighbors, the dad of Gary's friend, came over to talk to Gary about getting some car lights Gary had. He asked me where Gary was and I went ballistic, the poor man. I think I apologized to him, many times, afterwards because I totally felt bad I went crazy on him, yelling, "Gary? Gary is dead! Gary was killed in a car accident last night," then ran off crying. He had to feel bad at that moment, but he always told me it was okay. He felt terrible that he came over at the wrong time asking for him. Well, hey, life does go on for other people. People still do the things they need to, even though it feels like *your* life has stopped. Life does not stop at that moment! Remember that. It may feel like it has, but it doesn't. It has to continue and move on. The past is gone, but there is always the present and the future.

That took me a while to get over. I will admit it was nasty going through that day. Again, not to sound harsh, life had to continue. Life does go on as difficult as it may be, it must go on. I had to go through the whole wake and funeral, which were total and complete hell. I felt I needed to go through the wake for closure, to make this whole nightmare a reality. I needed to see my brother one more time so I could say goodbye. Well, from what I do remember and from what people have told me, I didn't go through it all that well. I really don't remember a lot of it, I guess.

I remember walking in to see the body before everyone else came to the wake. The immediate family gets first visitation privately. I remember seeing a drop of blood running out of his right ear. I lost it and at some point, I guess I was hanging on to Gary and I tried to climb into the casket at one point. I don't remember any of this! A family friend told me this. You can see how close I was to Gary. I put everything, but the kitchen sink, into the casket with him. I put my senior picture with a note telling him I would get the house someday and finish it. I put in Diane's picture, a couple cigars (in his suit pocket) and some tools. My dad finally had to say, "Enough."

Then, the 2 days of the wake were over and I was still living! Now, it was time for the funeral. I can't tell you anything about this day because I don't remember much. I do know it was the hardest day of all because it's the last time you see your sibling. Now that it's all over, I think I do remember walking down the aisle at the church, but I'm not sure.

I remember shortly after Gary died thinking maybe he went to save my mother's life. My mom, an alcoholic, would listen to Gary. He was her first-born child, her only son and they had that special bond. I would go back and forth with this theory, then figured again as with my first niece, that he was going to go anyway, like it or not. It was his time. I had to realize he was not taken away to save someone else, however, about 3-5 years after he died my mom did have an accident and had to go to the hospital. She received treatment and began seeing a psychiatrist for her depression, and has never had a drink since. I do not feel Gary died to save her, but I do think he gave some extra help up in heaven to help her out.

It was hard getting back into college life after Gary's death. I think a big part was I didn't want to leave my parents after they had just lost their son. They would be home alone now. I felt they needed me. I needed them. We needed to be close so nothing else would happen. I just did not want to do anything. I didn't know what I wanted to do with my life, but I did go back to school and continued on unsure of where I was going at the time. I knew things would eventually come together. It wasn't always easy. I knew Gary would take care of things and everything would get better. It always seemed to before and I believed it would continue.

A month after Gary had died; my girlfriend who I cheered with in high school died in a car accident. She died pretty much the same way Gary did; however, a friend was driving, lost control in the park and hit a tree. She was on the passenger's side; the same side as the tree and died of massive head injuries. Just like Gary. My parents didn't know how to tell me. How do you tell your child who just dealt with losing her brother, now to lose a friend and in the same way. They waited until after her funeral to tell me. They didn't want me going to it, feeling it would be too devastating. I remember being so angry with them. I should have had an opportunity to say goodbye to her. After a while, I was so glad they did not tell me. They were right. There would have been no way I could have dealt with that. I think it would have been so traumatic that I would have just lost it, literally. Instead, I wrote my friend's mom a note and she sent me the most beautiful note back. I still have the note and read it occasionally. It still brings me to tears.

After all this, I was on autopilot. One day a family friend called and we talked awhile. She started asking me questions about what I was going to take up in college. I told her, "I really didn't know." I was just taking classes and trying to stay in school. She told me I would be a good occupational therapist. I said, "Okay, that sounds good." So, off I went to become an occupational therapy assistant. I would help people who had been in accidents and survived. I would help people who had had injuries, etc. I would help people who lived through what my brother didn't live through. I would help them to live life to the fullest and as independently as possible. I found my niche. If I couldn't help Gary, I would help others in the same situation he would have been in had he lived. It was difficult to work with the men that were around his age. It always made me think about him; especially this one younger guy. He had dark hair, like Gary, and suffered severe head trauma. He lived the life of a vegetable. I worked hard to get him to be able to do something… anything. He never did. That always made me so thankful Gary did not live through his accident. It's a blessing he is with Diane, happy.

One day in college, I was having a bad day. I kept looking at Gary's picture, kept smelling his hat that smelled like diesel fuel and, all too quickly, losing his scent. I was in a daze. All I remember is walking to the window in my dorm room at Akron University and looking down to the courtyard where there were always people sitting around. I saw no one. No one that is, except Gary!

He was wearing the clothes from the accident and was looking up at me. I heard his voice as clear as day. I heard, "It's okay, Peewee.

Everything is going to be okay. I'm all right. I'm happy. You're going to be okay. I promise." Just as quickly, he was gone. I can only say I have never felt a sense of peace like the one I did at that moment. The hairs on the back of my neck stood up. I had goose bumps all over. Yet, I felt a warmth I never felt before. I knew I was not hallucinating. He was there. Gary's spirit was there and he was reassuring me that I was going to be okay. He was going to be there for me, still, as always, just not in person and he was okay. He was happy. I walked back to my desk, where I saw a picture I apparently had drawn of him. Now, believe me, I am no artist by any means. I can't even draw stick people. I have tried to draw that picture repeatedly, and cannot do anything near what I did it that day. Gary was the artist. He was with me before I saw him, drawing through me. That is what led me to the window. Led me to start living my life again, and you know what; I did from that moment on. Do I still miss him? Of course I do! Do I still cry because I miss him? Yes, especially on his anniversary, during the holidays and on his birthday. His birthday is always hard, especially for my dad. We always celebrated their birthdays together because they were only several days apart. Gary is still with us every day. There have been many instances when things have happened and I say a little prayer to him asking him to let me see something a little more clearly, so I can make the right decision. Then, bam, like a brick hitting me in the head, something happens making me realize what I need to do.

    I was fortunate I was able to see Gary and get that last goodbye, and him telling me I would be all right. How he would always make sure I would be okay just as he always had done before. Not everyone has this experience. I think you need to listen to those "cues," that little voice telling you something you don't always pay attention to. Maybe your sibling is trying to comfort you. Don't shun those feelings aside. Listen to them. Feel them. I have not heard of many other people seeing their sibling after their death, but I have heard people talk about dreams of their sibling telling them it's all right and they will be okay. Many people have some type of dream that is comforting. Listen to those dreams. Allow them to comfort you.

Some people are afraid to see their sibling. They do not want to see them because it scares them and makes it too real. It confirms their worst nightmare; their sibling is not coming back. Don't be afraid to see them is all I can say. Allow them to present themselves to you; even in a dream, if that is what they feel will help. Gary presented himself to me. My parents told me they talked to our priest because they were worried I was seeing things. He assured them it happens often when someone is very close to the deceased. The spirit comes back to comfort the loved one. After the conversation with the priest, they felt reassured I wasn't going crazy and losing my mind. With this in mind, don't be afraid to see your sibling. It is not a scary thing, not in the least. You feel a sense of peace and utter joy. I do recall feeling sad he was gone, but still happiness at the same time I saw him and heard his voice in my head, ever so clearly. It was as if, we were talking face to face, as if he was alive. That vision allowed me to move on with my life, really get back to school and studying.

People have asked me if I was scared when I saw him. As I have said, I was not. Instead, I felt peace. I often pray and talk to him. I ask if I could see him again. I never have since. I wish I would. I do feel his presence, especially in my grandparent's farmhouse. I feel my grandparents and great aunt who lived here, but I really feel Gary's presence the most. I always feel safe there. I had two instances where I had a nightmare at night. The first nightmare was about someone trying to break in the house through the front door. I woke up, but quickly fell back asleep. I then had another nightmare two guys were trying to break in and I tried getting to the door to lock it, but they pushed it open and I woke up. I woke up and figured, okay, Gary's trying to tell me something. I got up to check the doors and discovered I had left a candle lit. I blew it out and thanked him for making me get up. The candle was on a table by the front door. Another night, I had the same type of nightmare that someone was trying to get through the back door. This time I didn't play around. I got up right away to check and discovered I forgot to lock the back door. Now, if that isn't him helping me out, I don't know what is.

In this book, you will read other people's stories on how they coped with their personal situations of grief, but you will also read how three sisters handled their grief in their own way. The sisters are my two older sisters and me. I do honestly have to say my oldest sister and I have coped better and moved on with our lives, but my middle sister still fights with her grief, I think, on a daily basis. Writing her story made her realize she really hasn't been able to fully move on with her life. She is still "stuck" in her grief, thus making her daily life more difficult. She also is more introverted. Is that a precursor to not grieving, coping and moving on as well as my oldest sister and I have? I don't know the answer to that. I do have my feelings on it, but I do not know if this has been studied or not. My oldest sister, Jeanette and I are more extroverted, whereas, Gary and Laura were more introverted. Jeanette and I talked and talked to release our fears, stresses, anger, our loss, etc. I think Laura may have kept it in more, thus not moving on and having difficulty now after all these years. Thankfully, she has come to realize she does need to work on this area, thus, hopefully, improving other areas of her life.

It is amazing to me how three family members dealing with the same loss can deal so differently, and in some ways, so similarly. This leads to the fact everyone is an individual and deals with grief in their own ways; even family members going through the exact same trauma at the exact same time. Each of us were at different ages and stages of our lives, thus making our coping and grieving processes different for each other. Each of us also had different relationships with Gary. This makes a difference.

Not only was our grieving different; our motivation to move on was different. We each had different reasons to move on. Jeanette moved on for the sake of her unborn child. I needed to move on to thrive in college. Laura needed to move on, but is doing so more slowly in her own way...not always in positive ways.

My hope is by reading these stories; you will be able to find something in common to help you proceed through your grieving and coping process.

# CHAPTER TWO

# *Stages of Grief*

The amount of grief you feel when you lose a sibling is immeasurable. No one can describe the feelings you are feeling except someone who has been there and still each case is different. I have many friends who say they just can't understand what it would feel like to lose one of their siblings. When you lose a sibling, you feel like you are losing part of your own identity, part of your own history. They are the ones who have shared your childhood right by your side, even if you had a "rocky childhood."

Your siblings are your confidants, your best friends and even your enemies at times. However, you always have a bond, a bond that is difficult to describe. You may have had times you got upset with them and really didn't want to be around them, but you still loved them. That is just the way it is with siblings.

Until now, I have spoken of coping with the loss of a sibling when you had a good relationship. I have not yet spoken of the grief felt when you did not have a good relationship, or perhaps, you had a mediocre relationship and had not spoken to your sibling in quite a while. Possibly because you have been too busy or just hadn't gotten around to it. Maybe you didn't get to say goodbye. This is different from having a good relationship because you may have that extra guilt of not being close. You may have had a good reason not to be close to your sibling, maybe they were not the type of person you liked to be around. That's okay. You still need to go through the grief. You may need counseling in this situation. There may be deep feelings you have suppressed so as not to remember them. In order for you to really heal and cope with your loss, you are going to need to find this out and deal with what you have suppressed, so you may go on with your life. If you don't, it will eventually manifest itself in one way or another; be it in an illness or depression, with jobs or with your relationships. Please seek out the help you need to be able to live your life in a healthy manner.

If you didn't converse with your sibling because you never got the time to call and get together, it happened and there is nothing you can do about the relationship now. Learn from this, though. Learn not to take advantage of relationships. Don't wait for that opportune moment to call and get together, because you know there never seems to be an opportune moment these days. We are all busy. We just never seem to stop to smell the roses and appreciate our loved ones. When you are thinking of someone, call them. Get in touch with them. Make plans to get together because "someday" may be too late.

Many siblings I know don't really know each other because one was much younger or older than the other was and they weren't really around each other growing up. Maybe one was at college or moved out before a good relationship formed. This leads to another issue of grief, not having known your sibling and taking the time to get to know them.

According to Elisabeth Kubler-Ross, there are 5 stages of grief. They are denial, anger, bargaining, depression and acceptance. Everyone deals with loss in their own individual way, so these are just guidelines. Not everyone goes through all 5 stages of grief or in the order they are presented. They are just a way of describing what you may go through. In addition, some people may take a longer time to accept their loss than others may.

The first stage, denial, allows us to "survive the loss," according to Kubler-Ross. Everything becomes overwhelming, you feel numb and in shock. Nothing has any meaning to you. She states the denial and shock helps us to cope and make survival possible. In this stage, you start to ask questions, which is the beginning of your healing.

The second stage, anger, Kubler-Ross states is a necessary stage in the healing process. The more you are feeling the anger, the more it will dissolve and you will heal. I had a lot of anger. I was angry with God, angry with myself and angry with Gary. These are all normal in the anger phase. Do not feel guilty for feeling these. You need to remember these phases are part of your healing process. Anger is normal as long as it does not start causing damage to you or others.

The third phase is the bargaining phase. You make deals with God, or to whomever, to bring back your sibling. "I'll start going to church if you bring back my brother." "I'll stop drinking and smoking if only you bring her back." According to Elisabeth Kubler-Ross, guilt is often bargaining's companion. In this phase, we feel we could have done something to prevent the cause of death.

Depression is the fourth phase of grief. You feel empty, hopeless and helpless. When you think of it, the whole situation is depressing. We are allowed to feel depressed, but like everything in this world, the feelings need to be in moderation. It is natural to feel depressed after losing a loved one; however, not to the point we isolate ourselves, stop doing our daily routine, feel hopeless, helpless and stop living. That is not healthy. That is clinical depression and needs professional attention, so you can return to living your life, be happy and hopeful. Kubler-Ross also says, "If grief is a process of healing, then depression is one of the many necessary steps along the way."

Acceptance is the final stage of grief. Now, I know you're probably thinking, "Hey, she expects me to accept this death." Well, yes and no. Acceptance doesn't mean you say, "Okay, I'm all right with this; it is okay, it's good." What this stage means is you accept the "reality" of the situation, understanding this is a situation you can't do anything about, and you realize you have to learn to live with it and accept the fact they are not coming back. It doesn't mean you have to like the situation; it just means you accept it. To me, this was the most important step. I needed to accept my brothers' death and find peace with the situation. You will never like the situation, but you can find peace with it and move on, maybe even do something positive with it.

These 5 stages, and what they encompass, are all a healthy part of your healing process. When you go to alcohol, drugs, isolation, etc., which are not healthy, you need to realize there is help out there for you. If friends and family are not enough to assist you with the healing process, get the assistance of a professional counselor for help. Don't be afraid. Don't be embarrassed. Believe me, this is not an easy situation to get through, let alone accept. Sometimes we need an objective person who can listen to our stories with an open ear to really hear and understand what we are saying, or not saying to help us. You may be to the point you need mediation to help you get through it and that is okay.

I hear many individuals say they didn't have the opportunity to grieve because of situations where families expect everyone not to discuss the sibling, bring up their name or their memory because it was better left unsaid. "Let's not mention them, that way we don't need to think about them; that way we don't feel the pain." I can't even imagine this. I am so sorry to all of you who were or are expected to not discuss your loved one. A huge part of the grieving and coping process is to discuss your memories. The more you discuss them, the more you heal. In fact, I don't believe you can heal unless you feel and deal with the death. I am living proof. I talk about Gary all the time. I'm not obsessed with him. I just mention him as I would anyone else. Even after 28 years, I am still mentioning him! My advice for helping you grieve is to talk, talk, and talk. Don't hold in your feelings and memories...share them. If you feel like people are giving you strange looks, it may be your perception. You may think they are going to give you weird looks because you're talking about a dead person. If I ever had that happen to me, I have never noticed it, or just didn't care. I love talking about my brother and I am proud of him! (As if, you haven't been able to tell that!).

When you are a grieving sibling, it isn't unusual to do everything to try to help your parents. I did this by acting like my brother. You may feel as if you are their caretaker now. This is a normal, loving act, but you have to be careful they don't turn to you for everything. This can be helpful to your family, but it can be detrimental to your well-being and not allow you to deal with your own grief.

You need to take care of yourself and deal with your own grief before you are able to help others. You may be the one who has to take care of funeral arrangements after your sibling's death, so you may not get the opportunity to deal with your loss. However, it may feel that making the funeral and burial plans, etc. is healing itself. Talk about your sibling and realize that you are grieving just as much as everyone else is. You may need help also. Don't neglect yourself. Do things for yourself. Take a walk and enjoy nature. Remember old times, happy memories while you're communing with nature. Don't blame yourself. Don't feel guilty you're alive and your sibling isn't. If you are feeling guilty, take a nature walk and think about why you feel that guilt. Work through those feelings while you are walking. Walking really helps to clear your mind and it makes it easier to see things more clearly. Be selfish for a little while. Many times, you will find that you need to force yourself to do these things.

A very good book to read is John E. Welshons' book, "Awakening from Grief: Finding the Way Back to Joy." In this book, Welshons states when there is a loss in our life, we tend to lose track of who we are, what our lives mean and our happiness. We pretty much lose track of everything in our lives. He says, "If we can look at the losses in our lives a little differently, if we can change our perspective just slightly, we may see that within this experience lie the seeds of a new beginning, of a new life of a deeper experience of love and fulfillment than we ever imagined possible." He also states with every loss we come closer to being who we are meant to be, the life we are to have; if, we can look at the loss as something more positive, as a learning and growing tool. This is so true. It is difficult to see after a new loss, but really work on this one.

Welshons also states when we lose someone and we feel helpless and hopeless, we can feel that it is so difficult and impossible to even think that we will ever be happy again. But, we all have to deal with these difficult times that will essentially, "Make us or break us." It is how we deal with these difficult times that can actually bring us joy and peace. All the losses we go through, not only deaths, but loss of job, divorce, etc., make us who we are and who we are to become. When we have a loss, we need to try to dig deeper into ourselves and grow from the loss. This part is so interesting to me because it is hard to see through this in the beginning. However, think about what Welshons is saying here. The losses we experience and how we deal with them and grow from them makes us who we are to be. This is important to grasp.

I went through this, but I didn't know what I was supposed to do. After Gary died, I knew I was supposed to do something big, something important, but I just wasn't sure what. It took me years and years, and I lost a lot of money trying different things. I was almost 18 when Gary died and I didn't figure it out until my mom was getting a procedure done. I was in the waiting room with my dad when I had my revelation. At age 44! As you can see, I didn't pick up on it very quickly. But, I tell you, when I finally figured it out, I definitely knew that I had. A light bulb went off in my head and I never really did believe in that happening until it did. You will know when it happens. Now, I have my mission. To help others cope and heal from their losses.

# CHAPTER THREE
# *Coping*

Coping. What a word. In Webster's Dictionary, the psychological definition of the word "coping" means: "The things that someone does which enable them to handle a stressful event." People use different coping mechanisms they feel work for them and these can change as the healing process changes.

In reading this book, you obviously are in the process of either coping or trying to find out ways in which to cope or ways in which to cope better. Think of reading this book as your first step in the coping process. As Anthony Robbins says, "Think about what you are focusing on." Especially now while you are in the grieving and coping process. What are you focusing on this minute? What are you focusing on the majority of the day? Robbins says, "What you focus on you believe." Think about that. It's a pretty strong statement. If you are focused on something negative and/or stressful, change what you are focusing on. This is such a powerful thing to be able to do. If you can only empower yourself to focus on the positives of the situation, and the strengths you may have learned from your sibling, the wonders of life and celebrate your sibling's death, then, look what you believe in now. I am saying to live your life and focus on something positive to believe in. This is so amazing to me that I will repeat it. I want you to really think about it and give a 100% effort. "What you focus on you believe." Start focusing on something positive you want to become and to believe...NOW!

James Arthur Ray states this in a similar way, but in more depth. He says you need to focus on every area of your life. In his book, "Harmonic Wealth: *The Secret of Attracting the Life you Want,*" James gives you 5 areas of your life to keep in order. He gives you ways you can get all 5 areas in order to give you "Harmonic Wealth;" to be in harmony and truly happy. I suggest reading this book. He gives so many great things to do for yourself. This book is for every area of your life, not specific to coping with a loss, but it does definitely help if you follow his steps.

In Dr. Zeff's book, "The Highly Sensitive Person Survival Guide," he lists many coping strategies to help you cope with your loss. Dr. Zeff states you should create a daily routine. Get restful sleep, meditate, and do not rush. Use your senses to calm yourself. Listen to relaxing music, not loud noises that make you more jumpy and anxious. Limit your caffeine intake, but increase your water and herbal tea intake. Treat yourself, get a massage and try to start eating healthier. These are just some ideas you could incorporate into your day.

What he is saying is to reduce your stress level. By listening to calming music, staying away from high stress activities so you can allow your senses to relax and release. Eating healthier and in a quieter, calmer environment reduces excess stress. By allowing yourself to become calm and relax, you are allowing your mind and body some rejuvenating time to heal.

He also states you should develop a positive attitude towards your job, listening to quiet music, maybe have some calming, happy pictures around that increase your positive attitude, making you happy and helping to lift your spirits. If you are happy and relaxed, your co-workers will relate to you in a calmer, more relaxed way, thus being calmer and more relaxed at work. This reduces stress levels making it easier to cope at work.

Breathing exercises are also helpful. Take in a short meditation break. I will go over some techniques later. Just stop what you are doing, take a couple minutes to clear your mind. Just *BE* and relax. Clearing your mind is very invigorating to do throughout the day, allowing you to think more clearly and calmly. I started all this as part of my grieving process. It helped me grieve more peacefully and clearly. Then I dove more deeply into some of these other coping strategies to allow me to cope in a healthy manner during my coping process. My grieving and coping, I feel, were meshed closely together as being a combined process.

## Coping

The idea here is to do whatever you can to calm yourself and make it easier for you to cope with your situation. What calms you? What relaxes you? Take a couple minutes and think about this. Write them down. Picture yourself in a "happy place." Do you have a happy place? A place that makes you happy and relaxed, a place that puts you in the right frame of mind and makes you happy. Mine is tanning on a raft, hooked onto a buoy on Crystal Lake in Beulah, Michigan. Put yourself in your happy place and feel the sensations. Smell the smells. Feel the motions. Taste the tastes. Hear the sounds. See the visions. Are you there? Now, take a couple minutes and think about where your happy place is. When you have that place, relax and close your eyes. Smell, feel, taste, hear and envision yourself there, just relax. When you feel you have relaxed and are ready to come back to reality, open your eyes slowly. Know you can go there whenever you need to get away.

There are positive coping mechanisms and there are negative coping mechanisms. The negative, obviously are drugs, alcohol, depression, suicide, not living your life to your fullest and many more. Another is staying away from family members because it hurts too much or friends because you're too afraid to get hurt again. The stress alone of being afraid the next person you love is going to die is not healthy on your body or mind. Another reason it is much better to try to come to grips with your loss, both mentally and physically. Be healthy. Be happy and just *BE*.

You often hear of people not being able to cope with the loss or the guilt, and they get into a rut and start drinking and/or start taking drugs. This only makes everything worse. How can you heal and move on? You can't. You only put yourself in deeper and put yourself in the position to lose everything…your family, your job, your self-respect and your life! Go get professional help. Drugs and alcohol are not going to help you get over your loss. They only maximize all your negative feelings. It is your decision to live and move on or to feel sorry for yourself. You only get one life. It's your choice. It does take time to grieve, cope and come to an understanding about your sibling's death. Every person is an individual and takes their own amount of time in their own way to deal with loss. When it has been years and years, and your life is still where it was, or worse, shortly after their death, and you have pretty much lost everyone and everything in your life, or close to it, you need to take positive action. Maybe you have to reach your worst to be able to pick yourself back up and move on. If you can't help yourself, get someone to help you!

After Gary died, I started getting panic attacks, but was able to realize what they were. I did research on them and was able to talk myself out of them. I would mostly get them when I was driving and in closed-in situations where there were a lot of people. I just calmed myself and repeated, "Okay, everything is okay. Nothing is wrong. Nothing ever happens. Just relax." I would repeat this to myself and breathe because I knew nothing ever happened to me when I got them and nothing was going to happen. I just needed to calm down. That worked for me. I would talk to Gary to calm myself down also. They must not have been bad, but they seemed terrible when I got them. That lasted about a year; however, they dwindled, as I got better about talking myself out of them. This was my coping mechanism to get over the panic attacks. I used relaxation techniques and some guided imagery to help calm me.

Other coping mechanisms were talking about Gary. I told everyone about him. People listened. I did watch so that I wasn't boring people and going overboard with it, but I would bring him up when it fit into a conversation. I also did some journaling, but I was just starting college, so that didn't really last too long. It was helpful. I read a lot about different religions, mostly Buddhism and became interested in meditation. Meditation really proved helpful. It relaxed me and made me see things a little more clearly. This pretty much finished off my panic attacks. I would use meditation to relax and stop the panic attacks.

Another thing I did was keep a couple of his things in remembrance. Okay, at first, it was a lot of his things. My parents would say, "Hey, where is Gary's ring?" Oops, I have it. "Hey, where are those pictures of Gary?" Oops, I have that, too. The list goes on. I did get rid of things; however, I kept one of his work shirts with his name on it. I have a couple other things of his to hang on to, too. It was a good healing process to let go of the extra's I didn't need to keep. You just have to remember you aren't getting rid of the person. You still have your memories of them. You don't need all their "stuff" to remember them by. Remembering them is the important thing. Keeping their memories alive and celebrating the life they lived.

Another coping mechanism was throwing myself into college work. Going into the medical field for me really hit home because I knew I would be helping people to live more functionally after accidents, strokes, etc. That helped me feel like I was doing something in his honor. I also knew Gary would have been hurt if I didn't cope with his death. He always used to say, "When I die, make sure you water me." That sounds morbid, but he used to say it jokingly. I think he knew he wasn't going to live to a ripe old age. He always used to say he wouldn't live to be 55-years-old. Some people just know and I think he did. Another coping mechanism was going to the cemetery and "watering" Gary. When I go to the cemetery, I always talk to him for a while and say, "I'm watering you." In a weird way, it makes me feel good because I can see him giving me his smart-ass grin he used to give and that makes me feel happy knowing it is making him happy.

As I wrote this book, I started thinking about how I handled many situations. Going back to college was very difficult for me. I really wanted to stay with my parents and take care of them. Then, when I saw Gary in the courtyard at college, I really started to move on with finding peace with everything. I wonder, though, would I have gone through my grief and coping as quickly as I did? I honestly don't know. I do know that even before I saw him, I did feel something as though he was trying to help me cope. I think he knew that that was not enough to help me, so he showed himself to me to help me through it better. He never did like to see me sad or hurt. I feel he knew I was deeply hurt after he died and, I think, that was his way to help me. I guess I might have gotten through this, as

I did, just maybe not as quickly. Still, don't think by any means I am completely over his death. I don't know if you ever completely get over a sibling's death or anyone's for that matter, and I have said this many times and I will continue. I think by me seeing him one last time, it helped me say goodbye to him. Not a "Bye, I'll never see you again." It was a simple "Bye, see ya later." When I saw him, I was able to feel that goodbye. It put me at peace, and put him at peace I think, knowing now I would be okay. It was his final job taking care of me. Well, not really, he still continues to take care of me in many situations.

The loss of my brother has changed many things in my life. It chose my career. It helped me realize we are here to help and love each other, and not take anything or anyone for granted. My parents lost their oldest child, their only son. My mom did have another boy who was miscarried between my two sisters. I often wonder how life would have been different had he lived. After Gary died, I tried to become Gary for my parents. I tried to ease their loss, although, knowing no one could take his place. I tried to do everything he did for my parents. It was difficult. No one can take his place in any way, shape or form. He did anything for anyone and never asked for anything in return. I have tried to live my life as he did; helping others. This is why I wrote this book, to help those of you out there who have gone through the loss of a sibling, but don't know where to turn. If I can help even one person realize life can go on, I am carrying on Gary's way of life.

With coping, you have to consider the age you were when your sibling died. Different ages handle death differently according to your maturity level and understanding of death. I talked about how not being allowed to discuss your sibling usually presents itself in destructive behaviors; age also can. Toddlers and little children do not understand what death is about. They think it can be reversed and the sibling will come back home or they can call them. When you are a little older, maybe until 11 or so, and lose a sibling, you understand more of the reality of death...the finality of death. Children of different ages need to grieve and cope in their own way, and of their own understanding. They can start to act out more and misbehave to get attention. The parents may be grieving, coping themselves still, and are not realizing they are not giving the attention needed to their other children. If they are younger, they possibly have lost their playmate and need to cope day to day without their playmate. They have to relearn their playing habits.

If you were around 13 when you lost a sibling, you will act differently also. This age tends to either act out to get attention or the complete opposite, acts like nothing whatsoever happened. Remember, like adults, children will grieve, cope and act differently. With children, it is more related to their developmental stage and understanding of death itself. Everyone mourns in their own way and time, including children. They now need to find their own identity, as they only know their identity with their sibling.

Friends play an important part in a teenager's life. When you lose a sibling and you are a teenager, as I was, your friends play a major role in your healing process. Some people say it was hard for them to talk with their friends about their sibling. They felt they got blank looks as if their friend's just didn't know what to say to them. Sometimes you don't need your friends to say anything. Listening was important for me. As long as I could just talk about the accident and my feelings about the whole thing, I felt better. It is also important that teens know they can go to their parents or a close family friend to talk if they need to. They need to know the door is always open for them to talk, whenever they need to, on their own terms.

With teens, it is also important not to keep alcohol or medications out in the open. This is a fragile stage anyway without the added stress of losing a sibling. Teens are trying to find their own identity. When you lose your sibling, you are losing part of your own identity, making this stage even more difficult to get through. Alcohol and drugs are more accessible to this age group and they want to follow the crowd to be "cool." When you lose a sibling, the alcohol and drugs not only are a way of acting out and getting attention, but also to numb feelings and not feel the pain, or not to have to deal with the even more difficult identity crisis, especially when going to college. Alcohol is all around every weekend, especially at college parties. What a way to numb yourself; however, the reality is the numbing goes away, making things worse. You not only wake up with a hangover, but your pain is still there after the hangover is gone. It may numb the pain for a while and you may be having fun at that moment, but reality will soon be back.

Kids can be very mean when you are going through a death. You need to talk to people you trust. If you have a friend who cannot deal with you talking about your sibling, find another friend. If you have a friend who treats you badly, ditch them fast. It will make you feel a whole lot better. You don't need extra negative energy now. You need all the positive energy you can find. Many people out there *ARE* willing to help you and to listen to you. Remember that. There is always a light at the end of the tunnel, no matter how dark it seems initially. There always is! Sometimes you just have to look for it a little harder, but you will find it.

Losing a sibling in your adult years is another area not really discussed much in books. It seems like people are more concerned when you lose your spouse, parent or child, but when you lose a sibling and your both adults, you deal with your mortality. "When will I go?" "Will I be next?" Often times, this age group is dealing with helping parents cope and possibly their own children or children of the deceased sibling. They are considered the supporters and are not always given the proper time to grieve and cope themselves. My sister was dealing with finding out she was pregnant and that our brother died, all within a short period of time. She was dealing with the joy of being pregnant with her child and the grief of losing a sibling. I didn't deal very well with that one. It took me a while to be ecstatic about having a niece or nephew who was taking my brother's place. Eventually, everything came together as I realized the two really didn't have a connection. It was just his time. Gary wasn't taken out of this world so my niece could come in. She was an innocent bystander. This was a big step in my coping process.

I have read articles where psychiatrists say siblings need time to cope. They are expected to "Get over it," as I have been saying. If you need more time, take it. Another thing I had found is you need patience...patience with yourself, things, and the people around you. When you are undergoing such tremendous stress, every little thing seems to bother you more. Giving yourself time to just be by yourself and just *BE* can do a world of wonders to help relax you and your spirit.

Paul Chek from SelfGrowth.com states there are times when doing nothing may be better than doing something that is best for coping with your health and happiness. He states there are three choices that he teaches students to use. He states this for relationships, but I see where this is very helpful in coping with traumatic situations also.

The first choice he states is the optimal choice. This is, "The choice that produces the most favorable result for everyone involved." The second choice is the suboptimal choice, "The choice that doesn't get the best results for everyone involved." This type of choice is more selfish. It may benefit us, but also cause pain or discomfort to others around us. The third choice Paul Chek states is doing nothing, "The opposite of love is not hate; it is indifference." The fear of repeatedly failing in a situation may cause someone to do nothing. Sometimes this is the best choice for that person, for that situation and at that time. Say you are having a bad day and you need to get out of your depressed mood. You think, "Hey, I'll just go out for one beer. It will lift my spirits." Well, odds are it isn't going to stop at one beer and I can guarantee you, it won't make you feel better, at all! It doesn't take away the depression; it only masks it for a little while. This is where doing nothing would have been a better choice. This example isn't really where Paul Chek was going with this, but when I read it a while back, it made me think of how it could be turned a little and relate to this situation. Sometimes just sitting on the problem for a while and not doing anything about it is better. Later on, you may feel better. Go out for a walk. Get some fresh air. Talk to a friend. Don't make any life-changing choices when you are not in the right frame of mind to do so.

No matter at what age you were when you lost your sibling, the important thing is to deal with it. Talk with your family. Share your fears and sadness with them. It is not always easy, but it is the healthy way of dealing with loss. If you don't talk about your grief, about your sibling and express your true feelings and fears, these feelings will come out in other ways, such as in health issues or anger issues. If you are getting very angry with people and getting into fights, or not able to keep a job, thinking you just don't like it, feeling there is always something wrong, you need to address and talk about your anger. Maybe you are blaming yourself, parents, or a friend—someone who may have been involved with your sibling's death. If you cannot find a relative or friend, you care about and trust to discuss this issue, consider counseling. This anger issue needs to be addressed. The longer you cannot discuss your anger, the more it builds up inside leading to more damage to yourself and your life. These are all things to keep in mind as you are learning to cope. You may feel it is just part of the grieving/coping process. This is true; it may be. However, if it continues and gets out of control, you need to find help. This is not helping you or your loved ones. Again, consider what your sibling would want for you. Would they really want you to be dying inside yourself? Please, get help to deal with this anger.

Keep in mind everyone deals with death differently. You may get upset with a family member, thinking they don't appear to be sad over the death of your sibling. However, they may very well be coping also; they may just be handling it differently. Some people become more withdrawn, others angry, while others may become more extroverted, needing or wanting to joke around more. This may disturb you, but you do have to understand some people deal with stress by using humor. There is nothing wrong with this. Humor has been found to be very healing. Laughing releases what is called endorphins, which are a natural painkiller. They are also known to help alleviate anxiety and depression. Laugh away! Laughter is very therapeutic. Exercise has also been found to release endorphins. The important thing is to be dealing with the loss and not suppressing the anger, depression, possibly guilt, etc. So, let them deal with the loss with laughter. Don't shun them...join in. You might just feel better.

Be grateful you had your sibling in your life. It would have been more of a tragedy if you never knew them at all, if they were never in your life. Do me a favor. Every day, before you get out of bed and before you go to sleep at night, think about everything you have to be grateful for. Dwell on that, not on what you have to be miserable about. The more you dwell on what you are miserable about, the more misery is going to come your way. Since my brother's death, I have been searching for balance in my life. After reading many books on inspiration and motivation (The Secret, Jack Canfield books, Deepak Chopra and Anthony Robbins to name my favorites), I have learned what you think about and the energy you put out there comes back to you. If you are dwelling on the negative, your losses, how miserable you are and how guilty you are, negative energy/issues will come back to you. If you focus on being grateful instead of miserable, focusing on positive issues, striving for your goals, what you can do and are doing, positive energy will come back to you. Try it. What do you have to lose? Happiness? Will you be more miserable if you don't try it? I don't think so. At least give it an honest shot. I believed in this so much that I became a Life Coach. It was another way to help others live the life they wanted, to help them overcome their losses.

Writing this section of the book helped me remember so many extra things about Gary and things we did together. It makes me happy having them back to the forefront of my memory. Yes, I am still sad he is gone. Yes, I would love to have him alive and here with us, but I cannot do anything about that. All these memories stirred up in my mind make me happy. They are all a part of coping. I am very grateful for the time we had together. I am grateful for the relationship we had. I have no regrets, other than I didn't talk him into staying home that night, but how realistic is that? All of this comes to the point of the importance of keeping a journal. It helps to keep those memories alive and helps you to cope and heal.

This is one way to cope and deal with the trauma head on. I don't believe in sidestepping situations to make them easier. The only way you can get over something, even fears, is to just deal with it. If you can't do it by yourself, get help. It doesn't mean you are weak if you get help. I had a big ten-college football coach as a patient one time who yelled, "Coaches don't fail. We don't fall. Coaches aren't weak. We can deal with anything." You know what I told him. I said he was a human being and to get over it. Everyone has weak moments. Everyone can fail and/or fall at one time or another. It doesn't mean you are a weak person if you have a weak moment. You are a stronger person for realizing you need help and getting it, than thinking you are strong and not getting help. That to me is a sign of a weak personality. Someone who pretends they are strong, but really aren't because they don't have the strength to get the help they really need, and deserve to move on and live.

It can be easier to cope with seeing your sibling's friends, spouse and co-workers, depending on the way they died. It may still be difficult with things related to how they died. If they died in the hospital from a terminal illness, you may be afraid of hospitals and/or not like doctors and nurses. To this day, I hate seeing accidents, any kind, but especially car accidents involving telephone poles and trees. It is never easy anyway, but occasionally I think about how Gary died and what he went through those final moments. I still picture his car with him in it. You may have a related issue to your sibling's death that you have a hard time dealing with or want to stay away from. This is okay as long as it isn't something you need in life on a daily basis. If it is something like a bicycle, well, you can live with never riding a bicycle if they just make you nervous. If their death was related to a car accident and you just can't get into a car, well, you're going to need to cope because life is very difficult if you won't get into a car. You can't drive to work, be a passenger, etc. If it was difficult for you to see what they went through in the hospital and you are terrified with doctors and hospitals, you may need to get help if you can't get over it yourself. We definitely need doctors and hospitals. With things like this, you may need to talk to someone to get over these fears. There may be positives to fears also. Maybe they died from an overdose and you vow never to do drugs or alcohol. Those are good coping mechanisms and things to stay away from.

You know you have moved on and are okay when you see your sibling's friends, and you are no longer jealous they are alive and your sibling is dead. There is a period of time you go through that any time you see someone you associate with your sibling, be it a friend, co-worker, whomever, you have some jealousy. You think, "God, why couldn't it have been them instead of my brother or sister?" Then you feel guilty for thinking that. I really think this is normal, at least in the beginning stages of coping. For several months, I really had a hard time seeing other people Gary hung out with. However, as time goes on and you are learning to cope, that changes. I also think the more you are around your sibling's friends, the easier it is to cope. Again, you are facing the issue head on. If you continue to have these feelings about your sibling's friends, it is an unhealthy and dangerous anger. Obviously, you need to get immediate help. When you have moved on and are coping with your loss, you are excited and happy to see people your sibling associated with. It just makes you happy, not sad in the least bit.

After Gary died, I looked for some books to read to help me. The only ones I really found were more clinical, making me feel like I should be in a classroom. They almost made me feel worse. I felt like a clinical subject, not a victim of a sibling's death. I am happy to say over the years, there have been books written that to me are much more helpful, more realistic and meaningful to us. I also suggest reading any type of motivational book even if they are not related to death. Books by Deepak Chopra, Anthony Robbins, James Arthur Ray and Jack Canfield are a few of my favorites. If I am down about anything, if I start reading one of these books, it bounces me right back to where I need to be and focus on myself. If you aren't happy and able to live your life to the fullest, how are you going to help anyone else? How are you going to focus on your studies? On your husband or wife? On your children? On your parents? On your job? On your *LIFE*? You need to start focusing on healing yourself!

You don't have to agree with everything I say. I don't expect you to. I am just giving you options that helped others and me going through the same pain. Take what helps and forget what doesn't. Remember, everyone is an individual and handles every situation differently, and in his or her own personal way. What may work for one person may not work for another and vice versa. Therefore, you may have to try many different varieties of things to see what relaxes you, what helps *YOU* cope, what helps you deal with your situation the best. Try something. If it doesn't work then try something else. Anything else until something works for you. Give yourself credit, though, you realize you need extra help coping with your loss, otherwise, you wouldn't be reaching out for this book. So, be proud you are taking that step to move on. This is the first step towards getting your life back and realizing you can move on without forgetting your sibling.

In the end, only you can create the life you want, make the decision you need to move on to create a new life for yourself, one that is positive and totally created by you. Your abilities are unlimited. Do things that make you happy and bring you joy. Watch funny movies, read books that lift your spirits; get a makeover or do something good for someone else. Write down all the things you are grateful for in your life! Start by doing it right now. It just takes time. Give yourself the gift of time to heal and cope. It will come.

## CHAPTER FOUR
# *Negative and Destructive Behaviors*

When I first started my final draft for this chapter, I had to rewrite some of it because it sounded too harsh and negative, like I had an issue with destructive behaviors. In all honesty, I believe I did because of having my mother, her parents and an ex-husband who all had drinking issues. Now after rewriting this section, I have dealt with my father's unexpected death and burial on his 81$^{st}$ birthday, and being laid to rest right next to Gary.

I was very distressed with my father's passing and miss him, more than words can say, but he was ready to go. I have no guilt that he is gone. Like Gary, I spent every moment possible with him. We were best friends; just like Gary and me. Therefore, it was very, very difficult to cope with this sudden loss. I found myself coming home from work exhausted, taking care of two children and then going to my mother's house 2 to 3 nights a week to stay with her. My two sisters and I took turns every night to stay with her, as she has dementia and is unable to stay alone. I would have a glass of wine to relax while cleaning up after the kids, doing laundry and making dinner for everyone. Then one glass turned into two. One night, I needed a break, went out to dinner with my boyfriend, and wanted to have some wine to forget about my misery. Well, I had more than I am used to having and for the wrong reason. I came home and needless to say, had a major meltdown. That night I had a dream of my dad and Gary literally yelling at me to get off it and just do what I needed to do. This wasn't me and I needed to get back to reality to take care of the issues at hand. I literally woke up totally with a different attitude. I knew wine was not the answer and I had responsibilities I needed to deal with, not to mention finishing this book. Fortunately, this only lasted probably a total of a week, but to me it seemed like a lifetime. I can't imagine how it would be to feel like this for weeks, months and maybe even years. I literally felt sorry for myself and wanted to drown my sorrows. However, thankfully, either my conscience was getting to me or my father and brother were. I am the responsible one who is always there. I couldn't be the one to drown my sorrows. I have too many things to do and take care of. Thank you dad and Gary for bringing me back to reality.

This chapter has changed from being a little too harsh and not understanding destructive behaviors to living a destructive behavior and having a much better understanding of how it feels to get into a destructive behavior. You may say it was only for a week, but it was long enough to see how quickly and easily it is to be stuck in a destructive act. I now have a new understanding and can relate to this more. I only hope others can realize this just as quickly, if not quicker. There is more to life after death than hurting yourself.

There are many organizations available that you can just go to and receive help. Alcoholics Anonymous is probably one of the most well known. They have the 12-step program, which forms the foundation of many other support groups that deal with all different addictive problems. Use the internet to your advantage. Many different support groups out there can help. Why not use them and take advantage of getting the help you need and understand and learn the reasons why you got into the behavior.

People use addictive substances because it decreases their pain and increases their pleasure; what more can you ask for, when you are depressed with your loss? However, can't you get the same outcome from exercise? People continue to use the substance of choice more often and need more to get the same effects. Your job becomes affected, you start having blackouts of time, not taking care of your responsibilities and family and friends are put on the backburner. Then, one by one, you start losing these most important things in your life, throwing you deeper and deeper into your addiction to feel more pleasure and less pain, but instead you feel hopeless and helpless. It doesn't have to be this way. There is help out there if you will only accept it.

The first and most important thing is to realize and admit there is a problem. If you refuse to admit there is a problem, nothing positive is going to happen.

Abstinence/help is not easy. You need to be motivated to help yourself and need to face the problem head-on. The issues started the addiction (the death of your sibling, etc.) and need to be addressed. Once addressed, you can work on those issues to initiate the process of acceptance in order to begin your healing process. Then you can investigate with the help of professionals, family and friends, new, healthy and positive coping mechanisms to begin to heal.

As I mentioned before, some individuals grieve and cope with the loss of their sibling in a healthy way and move on. Not everyone goes through the death of a sibling learning some sort of positive lesson. Some people, depending on how old they were when their sibling passed, how the sibling died and how the family dealt with the sibling's death, will handle the healing process in different ways. In these cases, many either never cope with the loss or think they are coping with it by turning to negative behaviors that are destructive not only to themselves, but to their loved ones as well. In my experience and research for this book, it appears people losing a sibling when they are younger have a more difficult time coping. They may start to hang out with the "wrong" group of kids to get more attention, or become involved with self-destructive behaviors due to guilt because they are alive and their sibling is not. It also seems when the living sibling is from a family who is not coping with the death and do not talk about the death, pretty much acting like the dead sibling never existed, are the kids that have a more difficult time coping and are more apt to go towards destructive behaviors. Their behavior may change and they may start hanging out with kids they never would have before. They may start drinking, smoking, doing drugs and stealing. Teenage girls may start hanging out with guys they normally wouldn't have and start having sex. The females I have talked with and read about stated they grew out of these situations, but they still had difficulties, as they became adults. Some said it turned into problems with relationships or with their jobs. They figured it was unhappiness with their partner or job, constantly arguing or searching for something better. Through professional help/counseling, they came to realize it had nothing to do with the relationship or the job. They were unhappy with themselves and/or their situation. They never really accepted their loss to be able to move on.

As you see, destructive behaviors are not only with illegal and/or abusive substances. It can be self-destruction through improper diets (anorexia/bulimia), abusive relationships, etc. In the end, what needs to be understood is never having accepted your loss and dealing with it and/or other issues involved. Once you can understand this and accept there is a problem, then you can get the help you need. It is not easy, but with the help of family, friends and professionals, you can stay motivated to get your life back on track and live!

# CHAPTER FIVE
## *Sibling Rivalry*

**I**f you are having a difficult time coping and never had a good relationship with your sibling, there may be more to it than you realize. Think of why you didn't have a good relationship. Was it they just weren't the type of person you liked? Were they too good of a person? Did they always want to be the special one to your parents? Did something may be happen in your childhood you don't even remember, but you remember it made you distant and not like them? Sibling rivalry is common, however, it usually does subside in adult years; although, many continue with the rivalry through adulthood. Maybe you always felt you were competing with each other to be the better child; the one your parents loved more. Maybe you always secretly hoped something bad would happen to your sibling and really felt it inside, or even told them you didn't want them around or possibly even wanted them dead. Did they always have the better life? The better spouse? The better job?

It is normal to have some sibling rivalry. It is a part of being siblings and a part of growing up. Some rivalry may be good. It encourages us to be competitive and to push harder to get what we want.

Here is some food for thought…your thoughts and wishes did not kill your sibling or take them away; just as your thoughts and hopes of bringing them back and making deals with God cannot bring them back. Sure, you may feel like you are the cause, however, again, wishes and thoughts cannot take them away. It was their time to go…for one reason or another.

Maybe you did have something to do with your sibling's death. Maybe you were the one driving the car or were watching them, and ended up talking with some friends as they walked out the door and were hit by a car. Whatever the case, this is why they are called accidents. It was not intentional. This definitely will cause more guilt and weigh heavily on you. This makes it more difficult to get over the loss of your sibling because, first, you have to forgive yourself. If you cannot forgive yourself, it is going to be even more difficult to go through the grieving process, if not impossible. We can easily turn away when driving or turn away and have our sibling fall into a pool or run in front of a car or even have someone pull them into a car. Unfortunately, accidents happen and are a part of life.

No one can be perfect and prevent something from happening that may be inevitable. Please find it within you to forgive yourself and move on with the grieving process. Your sibling is already gone...don't kill yourself, too. Get help and live your life. You really should pull the courage up and out to discuss this grief and guilt with someone. This is a tremendous amount of guilt to be carrying around with you. This is not a healthy or happy way to live! It will not only hurt you, but all the people who love and care about you. If you cannot find it in your heart to forgive yourself for you, then do it for your sibling and your loved ones as a start.

I was blessed Gary and I had an amazing sibling relationship. I thank God and Gary for that every day. I was fortunate Gary and I really only had one misunderstanding, not even close to a rivalry. It was when he was having some major back problems and had to wear a back brace. From all the years of running heavy machinery and the heavy lifting he did, it was getting to him at a young age. One day, he was in a lot of pain and knelt by the refrigerator looking for something to eat. He had this thing with me where he would poke me right between the ribs, really hard. It hurt, but it was also really funny. Anyway, he was kneeling and I thought it was perfect timing for me to get him this time, but I didn't know he had the back brace on and that he was in pain. I got him all right. Right between the brace straps and he almost hit the ceiling. He yelled at me so bad that I ran into my room, crying. I felt terrible he yelled at me and even was a little mad, but I didn't know it was because he was in so much pain. I was young at the time and just didn't understand what he was going through. After a while, he apologized and told me why he yelled. I felt horrible. I think that was the only real fight, as short-lived as it was, and it was still very traumatizing to me at the time. I never wanted to hurt him physically or emotionally.

I hear so many stories of sibling rivalry and not getting along even into adulthood. I was brought up you are family and you stick together. I'm not saying we don't have issues also, we do. We have our moments where we may not all get along, but when it comes down to it, we will always love each other and be there for each other through thick and thin.

## CHAPTER SIX
# *Faith and Spirituality*

According to Webster's dictionary, the meaning of "faith" is, "A strong belief in supernatural power or powers that control human destiny." Many people having to cope with difficult situations such as death, disease, divorce, etc., have overcome their situations by having faith and/or believing in their faith so much it has been healing for them. During times of hardship and tragedy, our faith and spirituality are tested, making it stronger or weaker. When your faith is strong, it is an assurance or promise everything will be okay. Everything will turn out the way it is meant to. You trust God or your higher being to make everything okay.

We pray to God or our higher being for strength to cope and handle our loss, and to be able to live and move on without them in our life. Prayer is very powerful. Some say prayer can heal and conquer death. If you believe, have faith and pray to God or your higher being daily, and really feel and see what you want, God or your higher being will respond. The answer may not be what you want; however, it will always be what is best for you now and in the future.

We pray and have faith/spirituality to get and/or maintain peace in our lives to help us deal with our losses. Prayer is helpful in the healing process because it helps us to tolerate our pain, thus helping us find peace with the situation. Our prayers don't have to be the typical formal prayers, such as "The Lord's Prayer," the "Our Father," etc. They can be anything we want them to be. Make up your own prayer. Just talk to God or higher being and ask for strength, or whatever it is, you are particularly looking for at this point. I talk to God and Gary. I always make sure I state somewhere in my prayer I am thankful for what I have and for what situations I have been given in my life, even though I may not have liked them. They were given to us for a reason, to learn and grow from. There is a purpose for everything. I thank them for the strength these situations have given me. Each "cross" you can say, can either make you a stronger person or bring you down. I thank God for having them make me a stronger individual and that they are leading me to be the person I am meant to be. Gratitude is a very strong prayer for me. I am always grateful for every situation I am put in. Maybe not initially, but afterwards, you are able to see more clearly the situation and realize it happened for a reason. What did I learn from this situation? Ask yourself that. If you cannot find the answer yourself, ask in prayer. Ask your God, why was I given this? What am I to learn from this situation? Please help me see what I am to learn from this and give me the strength to move on and cope with this.

This somewhat ties in with what I shared on Elisabeth Kubler-Ross stages of grief. Many people pray and hold on to their faith to help them go through each stage. When we are grieving, we are able to get through some stages quicker than other people do, possibly because of our faith and spirituality. Others may take longer because they have no faith. There is definitely no time limit to grieving and healing. I do feel faith and spirituality does help to move the process along quicker. However, sometimes issues dealing with your loss are stronger than what you are able to recover from them. Meaning when you are unable to find peace and get over the fact your sibling will not come back or maybe you refuse to believe the way they passed on. These feelings may be stronger than we are, requiring help from a professional. Sometimes family and friends can help only so much. Sometimes they are limiting or blocking our healing process, and causing us to be stuck into the phase we are in. This is where prayer and faith again can help move us in the right direction towards healing.

You may want to start getting back into your religion/faith. You may want to do research on different religions you feel more comfortable with at this point in your life. You may also need or want to talk to your spiritual counselor/priest/reverend. Many people find comfort in talking with their religious leader to help them use their faith to deal with their loss. You may want to talk with friends of different religions and talk with their religious leaders for a different approach. There are many choices here to help you. Some people lose their faith after a loss and look more towards becoming "one with nature." This is also a very helpful spiritual "therapy." Communing with nature makes, many people feel closer to God or their higher being. Whatever works for you is the right choice, *FOR YOU!* Not for your parents, other siblings or family and friends, this is about your healing process, not theirs. They need to use whatever works for them, not what works for you. Again, as I have said many times, this is a very individual situation here. What works for you may not work for others in your family, and just the same as what works for your family very well may not work for you. No one needs to feel guilty when you are not all handling the situation the same. Everyone's faith helps them in their own way.

My oldest sister used faith to get her through Gary's death. I shunned away from it, but later on, I became much more spiritual and less "religious." After I saw Gary, it really made me think more about God and my spirituality and less about religion, and what others say God wants. I feel I go right to the source and pray directly to God. I thank God every day of my life and I am grateful he blessed me to have Gary in my life for the length of time I did. It really would have been a tragedy had I never had him as a brother. As the old saying goes, "It is better to have loved and lost than to never have loved at all."

I am a strong believer in the power of body, mind and spirit. What you believe in your mind will either make you or break you. If you have negative thoughts, it will take its toll on your body with health issues and diminish your true spirit/spirituality. You need to find a balance in each of these areas to heal. Look at all the people that were told they will never walk again or will not live to see their children marry, etc. These people who have a strong mind, body, spirit connection and faith believe they will walk or believe, and know they will see their children marry and have children. Those ones are unstoppable. They have such an immensely strong and positive mind/body connection that they don't believe they will never walk or see their children marry. They aren't in denial. They just truly believe they will overcome their obstacles and envision their goals. They are the ones to defy the doctor's words. This is what I am talking about in mind/body/spirit connection. You truly have to believe you can get along with your siblings and truly believe if they have died, that you can go on without them. You have to. You have a life to be lived to the utmost of your ability. Use faith to move on.

## CHAPTER SEVEN
# *What You Can Do!*

Do me a favor. Write down what you have been thinking about today. Has it been mostly negative thoughts or positive thoughts? If they have mostly or all been negative, you need to start thinking about positive things. Things in your life you want to do. It can be to come to peace with your sibling's death. That is a big one. Think about it. What are small steps, small goals, you could do to help you do this? Write everything down. Write down your goals. Make long-term and short-term goals. Give them deadlines. Make them positive. As an example, I will own my dream home on Crystal Lake by July 21, 2010, at 12 noon. Focus on things *YOU* want in life. Remember, what you focus on you believe.

Maybe you need to do some things to put closure to your sibling's death. Maybe go visit where they were when they passed away, talk to the person they were with, forgiving someone who was involved, or forgiving yourself maybe. That could be a goal. Maybe you need to talk with a counselor, a psychologist or psychiatrist. That could be another goal—to make that call and make an appointment. Are you getting the feel for this? I hope so.

Another area I have gotten interested in because of Gary's death is motivational books. I have also studied in Life Coaching and Grief Counseling to help others realize we are in charge of our own lives. What you put out there comes back. If you are always upset and can't move on, you won't move on. Believe me. I hear it all the time. However, it is a choice you consciously make. Remember your sibling in a healthy way, not in a dangerously unhealthy way. Would your sibling really want you to live mourning about them and not living your life to the fullest because of them? Maybe, I don't know. I have to think that the majority of people would not want that. It doesn't mean you are a bad person if you move on. You don't need to feel guilty. I never told my family I felt I was to blame for Gary's accident. I held it in. I believe that started the panic attacks and claustrophobia. I just had to remember he would not have wanted me to blame myself. I had no control over his death. It was his time. It would have happened one way or another. We cannot dwell on the past. Instead, we need to move on, to live. I know what you are probably thinking, "No, I can't!" *YES, YOU CAN!* You are in charge of your life. Only you can make the choice…the decision to move on. You are the one to say what your life is going to be like. No one can make your life better, but you! What are you waiting for?

One of the things I learned in my studies with life coaching is you need to write down 3 things you are going to do each week to help you reach your goal. Maybe one of the things would be to mention your sibling's name, to talk about them once a week. Maybe not talk about them all the time. To cut back talking about them to 5 times a day versus 50 times a day. Another item may not be related to that at all. It could be a goal to call the local college to take a class you have wanted to take for years and haven't had the motivation. Write these things down, and do them! Put your thoughts into action.

Put yourself into a quiet room with a pen, a pad of paper and write. Write anything that comes to your mind. It may be related to your goals, it may be related to your sibling or to nothing even remotely close. Just write. Look at what you wrote and look to see if you found answers or new ideas. Writing can help heal. Keep a journal of your thoughts. This is a wonderful way to clear your mind. Focus a couple of minutes on a problem you are looking to find a solution for and then just start writing what comes to your mind. You may find you come up with answers to the problem or get ideas you didn't know you had. Do this daily or weekly. Whatever works for you. You may find healing in it and you may find endeavors you didn't know you had. Get them out and put a plan into action.

A fun thing to do is to write down 50 to 100 things you want to achieve before you die. They can seem silly or unreachable…it doesn't matter. They are yours to keep; nobody else has to see them. Then, look over these and pick the top 10-20 you really want to work on right away. Which ones can be short-term goals? Which ones can be long-term goals? Write them down positively and with a date to achieve them by. Put a copy in your purse or wallet, put a copy by your bed and maybe even on your computer. Somewhere you can see it readily. I typed mine, put a border and framed them. Add new ones as needed.

You can also make a vision board with pictures and phrases of goals you want to achieve. Take a picture being happy and smiling. Put a picture of your dream home, etc. This helps because you can actually see daily the goals you want to achieve.

Goals are a way to help you heal. Focus your energy not on the past and your loss, but on the positives and your future. For an example, I read one woman's brother passed away because he had a mental illness and was not taking his medications, and committed suicide. No one in her family ever really understood what he was going through. She turned her negative into a positive. She learned about mental illness and became a counselor for people with mental illness. How wonderful is that? Now she can help others who may not know about mental illness and can possibly help their family members see the signs, before it is too late. She is doing this in memory of her brother.

As I have mentioned before, you can meditate. Many people really don't understand meditation. It's not easy to master, but it is easy enough to do; I can assure you of that. It takes many years to do it correctly, but there are still many benefits of starting to meditate. The most difficult type of meditation for me is to just empty your mind. I can do it for a couple minutes, but then thoughts keep coming to mind. When this happens, you just address them and move back into emptying your mind. It does get easier, but this one is difficult for me; however, there are many other ways to meditate.

An easier one for me is to sit on a chair, hands in your lap, usually palms facing upwards, and focus on a candle or an image. Soft, soothing music is a nice affect. Just focus either on the image or on the flame of the candle. I have read in the past about the candle and it is easier for me than just closing my eyes and clearing my mind. If I focus on the candle flame and listen to the music, it is easier to clear my mind of clutter. Sit for 10 to 20 minutes to start and then work it to 30 minutes daily. I try to make meditating a daily habit, but that doesn't always happen. This is one of my goals I am working on. I try to do it when my kids are not home because it is too noisy for me. Prior to starting the meditation, focus on an area you want to receive answers and ask for help to those answers. Then, focus on the flame and clear your mind. Be open for your inner self to find those answers.

Another way of meditating is to focus on your breathing. Again, prior to meditating, focus on what you want answers to. Then, take a breath through your nose, allowing your stomach to expand. Feel it with your hand to make sure you are breathing correctly. Breathe out and allow your stomach to go in. Focus on your breathing. When you have a thought pop into your head, just give it a quick consideration and allow it to leave. Focus again on your breathing. Soft music always helps me with this one also. I like this one too because I can focus on the breathing and thoughts don't pop into my head as much by focusing on the breaths.

There are so many options out there for you. What you need to remember is YOU ARE IN CHARGE OF YOUR LIFE. You need to make the choice if you are going to continue to mourn and be stagnant in life or do you want to grieve your loss, knowing they would want you to live your life as best as you can. Realize they would not want you living in a negative way, not getting on with your life and even possibly blaming yourself for their death. Believe me this is no way to live your life. They would not want you placing blame on yourself and not living. Remember accidents happen. We don't mean them to happen. Their life is gone. Why should yours be gone also? Do not allow them in death to enable you. Maybe they did in life, but do not let that continue. You are in charge. I do not mean to make this sound harsh. If you are having a difficult time coping, I have said it time and time again and will continue, see a counselor, psychologist, psychiatrist, grief counselor or grieving group. It is just not healthy emotionally, physically or spiritually to do otherwise. Meditating can help alleviate some of this pain. Why not at least try? Give it an honest effort. You will never know if it works or not unless you try. Go on the internet. There are so many different web sites to learn meditation from. Check them out.

If you feel guilty, try to turn it into something productive. Turn it into something healthy. What did they die from? Is there any way you can turn it into something useful? Can you become a motivational speaker for this cause? Can you learn about the disease, etc. and help others going through the same issues cope better? Can you volunteer your time in shelters? Be creative. Speak at schools. Educate yourself and others on drinking and driving. Turn the negative energy into something positive your sibling would be proud of. What did they like to do? Maybe they loved to work out. Maybe that would bring you comfort in starting an exercise program like they did and benefit from.

It is also very, very important to get a good night's sleep. Getting proper rest, nutrition and exercise are all very important to you especially when going through a traumatic event. Sometimes it is very difficult to get good sleep. Your mind keeps racing with thoughts of your sibling. Then you start thinking of all the things you should do and haven't done because of no motivation and/or depression. All these thoughts, plus many others going through your mind, leave you a very non-restful night with no sleep and having to get up in the morning even more distraught and exhausted with absolutely no energy to deal with your daily life; each day getting harder and harder to mentally and physically deal with.

A good way to try to prevent some of this is to sit down before you go to bed and write down all your thoughts, and I mean all your thoughts; not just thoughts about your sibling, but of everything going through your mind. Write down things you know you should take care of. Write a list down. Maybe go one-step further and write down what things you will, or at least will attempt to take care of the next day or during the week. All those thoughts can now relax in your mind knowing you have taken care of them. They are on paper and you will not forget them. Now you can go even one-step further. By your bed keep a notepad and pen, and when a thought pops into your mind, write it down and let it go. Close your eyes and think about the things you wrote down on the paper. Picture yourself by a river with the water running at a steady flow. Picture everything written on that piece of paper and in your mind and picture yourself putting the paper in a bottle with a cork. Now, place the bottle in the river and watch all your thoughts float away down the river. Let those thoughts just flow out of your mind as they float down the river. Keep picturing this until the bottle has gone beyond your sight. Keep those thoughts in the bottle and have a restful sleep.

I will go into more detail on different exercises to do in the next part of this book, "Moving On." It will take you forward in your healing process and coach you through to live your life. I will help you look at where you are now; where you want to go and help you get through to reach your goals.

# CHAPTER EIGHT
# *Stories of Hope and Inspiration*

In this chapter, you will be reading stories from other people just like you, who have gone through possibly the same type of scenario you have with the loss of your sibling. It may be very different. Either way, you will read their stories and see what they went through and how they have coped or are coping. Some may still be in the healing and coping phase, and, yes, some may have even found something positive out of their situation. This is my goal. For you to find some hope and peace with what others have gone through and maybe help you to realize you are not the only one going through this situation, and you can learn to move on and live your life. You may also learn your life is to turn in a very different direction, one of happiness and acceptance.

## Pat's Story
## "My Mom's Story"

My mother's name is Pat. Actually, Frances Anastasia Divis-Stack and she was born on March 19, 1929, a twin. To the best of my mother's recollection, my grandmother was suffering from a flare-up of malaria she contracted on her honeymoon, suffered a ruptured appendix and went into labor. She delivered prematurely two girls, Anastasia and Frances. My mother, Frances, was older by approximately 1 minute, weighing in at a whopping 3-1/2 pounds. Her sister, not as fortunate, weighing in at 1-1/2 pounds, lived only a few hours and was baptized in preparation of her death. Her little lungs and body were unable to take the toll. In 1929, it was a miracle she even lived at all or that my mother made it, and is presently 80-years-old and still kicking. Their nicknames were to be "Patsy and Nancy."

My mom says, even to this day, she thinks what it would be like to have had a sister. She said she thinks more about it again now that she is older. She has two younger brothers, but always wanted to have her sister with her. She would have had done things with her that they both liked to do and even would have gotten to switch clothes and do different things together. When she was little, she used to cry that she missed her from the bond she still had even though her sister did not live. She didn't know her, but being a twin, she knew there was a piece of her missing. That something just wasn't there to be a part of her. She never even had a picture of her to see what she looked like. This always bothered her and still does. She does have the tiny, tarnished cross that lay across her tiny little coffin, still in her jewelry box. When we were little, mom would take it out and show us, telling us all about her "little sister" who was all of 1 minute younger than she was.

The doctor's were surprised and my mom says they called my grandmother a "miracle" because she lived through the delivery and surgery. She stayed in the hospital for quite a while. My mom does not remember how long her mother stayed in the hospital, but mom stayed in an incubator and in the hospital for what she thinks was at least 3 months. She did suffer and has suffered in her older years from some pneumonia because of inadequate lungs. Overall, rather healthy for what she went through and in her words, "tiny, but pulled through!"

## *Kelly's Story*

This story is one all-too-often heard…one about young adults getting together and having a good time. On the way home, they get into an accident and lose their precious young lives, way too early. This story, just like all the others, is so difficult. They're young and alive, then just as quickly gone. However, I still believe, for a reason. We may never know the reason or like the reason, but there is one, just the same.

Kelly is still in the coping and healing stage, but moving forward. She has found you can move on; not easily, but you can. She has been able to learn from her brother's experience, to make family and friends a priority. It sometimes takes a tragedy to make us realize how important all the people in our lives really are, and after a death, we really do tend to appreciate others around us that maybe we weren't appreciating as much as we could have. We tend to be so busy in our lives that we don't take the time to say, "I love you" as often as we could or would like to.

## Kelly's Story...
## Bret William Scanlon
## March 25, 1981 – March 31, 2002

My brother, Bret Scanlon passed away March 31, 2002 on Easter Sunday in a tragic accident at the age of 20. Bret was a college student at the University of Dayton where both my parents and my uncle had gone. They were so proud he chose U.D.–"Go Flyers."

Bret was on spring break and for his 21st birthday gift; my parents took him and his friend to Las Vegas. They had a blast! They came home on Saturday, March 30th. That evening, Bret and many of his friends from "home" (high school) got together at a local hangout (just down the street from where we grew up), to reunite and watch some basketball. They had a great time getting together and catching up! When the evening ended, Bret and his friends headed home. One friend drove with another in the front passenger seat and another in the back behind the driver, my brother, Bret was in the back behind the passenger seat. The driver began to speed on the winding street, almost "home" to my parents' house, when he lost control of the SUV and crashed into a mailbox, and then a tree in front of a house. From what I was told, my brother died at the scene. Life Flight came and flew him to the hospital, but it was too late. He had "head trauma" we were told. The front passenger lived for approximately 8-10 hours and then died. The boy next to Bret in the back lived with injuries and the driver lived without injuries. Until this day, going to my parents' house, having to pass where the accident happened is very difficult. I don't know how my parents do it every day.

While Bret was with his friends that evening, I was at home with my daughter Kayla, husband Russ, and best friend Tricia and her daughter Mariah. We were coloring Easter eggs. I also made a birthday cake for Bret, as we were going to celebrate his 21$^{st}$ birthday. I hadn't seen Bret since Christmas and I was looking forward to seeing him.

That night at around 3:00 a.m., I received a call from my parents. Just by the phone call I knew something was wrong and then hearing my dad's voice trying to say, "Bret was in an accident," I knew Bret was gone. I felt like I would die, too. The feeling I had was so empty and was for so long. I continue to have an empty spot and always will–so not prepared, as no one is. I remember after my parents called, my little girl Kayla, four-years-old, could hear me crying Bret was gone. She grabbed a photo of him, gave it to me and said, "Here, Mommy, here he is. Here's Uncle Bret, he's okay." I will never forget that night. I think about Bret every day from when I get up in the morning to when I go to bed. A life so worth living is gone.

My brother's passing away changed my life in so many ways. Negatively, I am nervous every day someone else in my family or close to me is going to die. I am cautious of everything and too over protective, especially with my daughter Kayla. I always feel like something tragic is going to happen and it can't be good to feel like this.

Positively, when Bret's passing happened, I was 27-years-old. I grew up real quick making family a number one priority. My mom, dad, sister, husband and daughter became much closer to me. My mom and I talk every day, sometimes 3 times a day. She's my best friend. It made me realize how precious life is and it can be taken away just like that.

I am extremely sensitive when discussing people's feelings and can't seem to keep my emotions under control. Meaning, I could cry just by a sad or emotional thought or listening to someone's sad story. I try to hide it. I never was a 'crier' or an emotional person before Bret's death. Now, I feel like I have no control over my emotions. I do feel alone. It's hard to talk about it or I'll cry. I do like to talk about Bret because he's part of my life and I don't want him ever forgotten.

I'm sorry to say, I don't think I have coped with this. I was worried about my parents and sister, and felt like I had to keep control and make sure they were okay, and not worrying about me. Now, 7 years have passed, I don't know if the feeling I'm feeling is "normal" or "right," or if I really need help. I do know I could just cry talking about Bret. I really miss him.

I guess if I were going to give advice to someone coping with the loss of a sibling, I would suggest keeping family close, maybe talking to a professional and continuing to keep your life going. Always keep your memories and talk about them.

Being approached about "Coping with the Loss of a Sibling" and asked to discuss my experience really made me happy. I never really had a chance to discuss my feelings. I feel good talking about my brother and the great person he was. I don't want him forgotten and I am so proud of him. I miss joking around with Bret. We had so many laughs and I think the same sense of humor. He had everything going for him. He loved life and was someone everyone loved to know and be around. His personality, smile and humor were unforgettable.

I will always be proud he's my brother, a great student, athlete, friend, and most of all, uncle, son and brother.

~~~~~~

I read Kelly's story and it gives me chills. The ironic thing is I knew the other person involved in the accident that passed away. This book has brought some interesting situations into my life. Kelly and I felt our meeting was meant to be and I feel the idea of this book brought us together.

It is interesting to note also how Kelly felt the need to take care of her parents, just as I did. We tend to want to try to take control and protect parents, and the remaining siblings and family members. This is common in sibling deaths.

## Michelle's Story

All deaths are difficult to deal with, but when they are so violent, it seems almost impossible to cope. In this next story, you will see how a family's determination solved a mystery, so all loved ones could finally get the answers and begin their healing process.

### Michelle's Story...

My brother, a heavy drug addict, lost everything and ended up back home. There didn't seem to be any hope in sight anytime soon for him. It happened in June 2004. He left the house one day on a Saturday morning and never returned.

We called in for a missing persons report a few days later. My dad and I did all the work the police wouldn't. We asked around, retrieved his cell phone bills and contacted everyone on the list. After a month of looking and gathering notes, we turned all the evidence over to the police and an arrest was made on the information gathered. The person was served 18 years to life. My brother, we found out, shot six times in the back and his body dumped in a ravine and burned. Had my father and I not had the drive of love and the promise I made to my mom that I would find him, who knows.

I feel for the people on the news looking for their loved ones, I could go numb. I couldn't imagine not finding my brother. To this day, I know he was with me giving me clues and keeping me up thinking of the people we questioned. I think how else could we have done this and gotten enough to convict a murderer. About a month after we found and buried him, I left my husband of 20 years, moved home with two kids, a part-time job and no car. I got an apartment after 2 months. My brother had a newer car my parents gave me and never looked back, just forward. I have a new home next to my parents, a daughter that is finishing her Associate's Degree, only after being out of high school 1 year, and a son who is a great kid (wins student of the month for kindness), and an ex-husband who is now in jail for some time and not his first since I left. The kids and I are as strong as can be. And through all this, I had cancer in between.

Live the best while you can, never look back, and always move forward. I miss my brother deeply and think of him always. It helps to think he is at peace. His demons are gone and he is in good hands. This is how I deal with him being gone.

I learned a valuable lesson at his expense. His loss of strength is what I gained. Looking for him for that month, I don't think I had a real mourning process. My drive or way to deal was to find him. I visit him on holidays. On birthdays, I bring him balloons!

~~~~~~

As you can see, Michelle and her family had to not only deal with their loved one's death, but also had to find his body and his murderer. I found such strength and courage in this story. Michelle not only found her brother's murderer, but also found herself in the process. She moved on with her life in a big way, doing what she had to do. It gave her the strength and courage to fight her cancer and really live!

# *Geneva's Story*

In Geneva's story, her faith and her husband helped to give her the strength to get over her brother's death, and she was able to make positive changes in her life because of it.

### Geneva's Story…

Geneva's brother was only 18-years-old when he died. He died on December 20, 1968. His death changed her life in a positive way in she now always gives hugs. She writes letters and talks often. She found how to remember the joys always.

She found great support from her husband during her healing process. She used this experience to make positive changes in her life by living every day to the fullest and trusted in God. "He will help you make it through all things." Her suggestion to help others going through the same experience is to Trust in God.

~~~~~~

From Geneva's story, you can see her strength and faith in God. Finding strength in God has helped many cope and heal. Knowing their sibling is in God's hands and in a "better place."

## *Irena's Story*

Losing a sibling when you are an adult is hard enough, but when you are a little child yourself just starting to understand what death means, it is hard to grasp what is really going on. Irena had to deal with losing her little brother and had to grow up and learn how to cope her whole life.

Irena lost her brother, John Charles Blake, Jr., who died on January 10, 1995, when he was 3 years, 5 months old from RSV, which is a major cause of respiratory illness in young children and in rare cases can lead to death.

### Irena's Story...

Well I was 11-years-old when my brother died. Our little sister was only four months old. It took 6 months to find out why he died. Nobody got to say goodbye because he was already brain dead when the paramedics got there.

Because of this event, I still suffer from PTSD (post-traumatic stress disorder), OCD (obsessive-compulsive disorder), depression and anxiety. It has been 14 years; I am 25-years-old now. I am in therapy and take multiple medications daily.

My sister, who was four months when he died, still feels the loss. My sister, who was born 2 years after he died, also still feels the loss. I see my whole family suffering still and I hate it.

I have trouble in relationships because I am always afraid of loss. I worry about some illness killing my kids, husband, sisters, parents and others. I worry about car accidents, natural disasters or freak accidents happening to someone I love.

After my brother's death, my family functioned so poorly and sloppy, and now I am OCD about being on time everywhere. This can be a good or bad thing.

I am a lister. I have lists of lists because of the above-mentioned problem with my families past with functioning.

I would not be who I am today if it weren't for my brother's death. I am a very strong person, but with a few quirks. I could have turned out much worse. I did many negative things to others and myself after he died. However, in time, I learned how to do other more productive things. I am doing things now like yoga, art and knitting to cope with anxiety. I am also on therapy and medications to help me cope.

I had to grow up quickly after he died, but I am a well-functioning adult. I am married with two kids of my own. I did worry a lot when my kids were babies that they would die from RSV also, but my therapy helped me get over that.

As far as using this experience to make positive changes, as I said, it took me a while to figure out positive things are better than negative ones. I try to live day to day—enjoy every day because life can end anytime. I want to cherish every second.

I won't let others talk badly about their family, especially siblings. Only because they don't know what it is like to lose one.

As for what you can do to help you get through this, find someone to talk to and you have to like talking to them. And, DON'T TAKE ANYTHING FOR GRANTED!

As you can see, Irena has had a very difficult time; however, she has been able to find positive aspects in her brother's death. She is now a stronger person because of it and has learned how precious life really is. She learned to cope using positive strategies such as the yoga, art and knitting. Many people who have not experienced death do not understand how it feels when someone close to you dies. All of us, who have experienced this, really do appreciate our family and friends on a much deeper level.

Yet, still, Irena is going through the coping process. When you lose someone when you are so young and don't even have your own identity yet; it really does take longer to learn who you are and how that death has changed you and to cope and learn over the years. Irena has come a long way and continues to cope and heal.

## *Laura's Story*

My name is Laura. My sister, Roberta, is the author of this enlightening book regarding the loss of a sibling.

We lost our brother, Gary, at the young age of 28. Roberta and I had both come home from the University of Akron for the Labor Day weekend in 1981. Gary worked on our grandparent's home for a while and then decided to go listen to his "favorite" country music. That night turned out to have "happy thoughts" and "bad endings!"

It was Friday, September 4, 1981. Gary said to me, "Laurie, I'm going out for a little while. I'll be home by midnight." Mom and dad had just gotten the news our sister, Jeanette, was going to have a baby. As the saying goes, "One life is taken and another is born." Our brother was taken that early September 5th morning, but we have gotten a beautiful niece (Krista).

About 2:53 a.m. is when the accident happened. Until this day, I still wake up at that time. At around 2:45-2:50 a.m. (09/05/81), Dad and I both sat looking out the front window. We knew something happened because Gary always called. At approximately 4:25 a.m., Saturday morning, the phone rang. The most heart-wrenching words, "Do you have a son by the name of Gary M. Stack? He has been in an accident. PLEASE come to the hospital now." We don't know the cause and never will. They say he fell asleep at the wheel! Yeah?

Our mom and dad came home before 7:00 a.m. (09/05/81). We waited for Gary to get out of the back seat. He didn't! He was never coming home. My only brother was gone. As I write this now, I am crying. I need to take a break! This day was one of disbelief and "DEVASTATION!"

With Gary's passing, I have learned to live one day at a time and to appreciate it. You need to cherish every minute of the day—whether good or bad.

I am the only one in our family to have two boys. My oldest, D.J. (16), is a lot like my brother (or is compared to him). There are a lot of similarities in their actions and interests.

Twenty-eight years have gone and I still have issues coping with it. I pray, cry, laugh and share memories with my children. My little one, Joey, constantly hears that Uncle Gary would wake up in the morning and say, "Quack, quack," and the ducks would answer back. Joey is also aware that Sparky, Gary's goat, chased me up a tree. Thinking of all the memories of my brother is what helps me cope/handle the loss.

I keep wondering if the experience (the loss of our brother) has made positive changes in my life. Well, I miss him. Gary's death, that is the first I have ever referred to his loss as that, has made me think about things. I may go day-to-day, but the children come first. The boys both have extra school/sports activities in which they get our support. I am the first to say I am over-protective. They need to learn and grow. The boys need to go out and seek the positives and possibilities available to them. Gary strove for many things. He worked long and hard. Once he got home, he still worked. I only hope my children will follow Gary's example of hard work, as Gary followed our father's footsteps.

To anyone that has experienced such a loss, please remember to cherish what you had. You can think of the good, bad and the ugly that might have occurred. These individuals, that have left us too early, are watching over us. So be Good!

Gary, your life was cut too short. God apparently had a special place and intentions for you. When you left, a part of me went with you. I'm sure you know this (up there), but you have four nieces and two nephews. My 16-year-old is like you, Gare. Joey treasures you even if it is only in pictures. We miss and love you, Gary.

Love you,
Laurie

After reading everything, I realized I definitely have not gotten over the loss of my brother. As my son, Joey read this I cried and cried. How do you deal with it? Apparently, I have not been able to figure out how. I love my family and try to do the best I can. I'm still missing something, but *WHAT*?

------

In reading Laurie's story, you can see she is still in the process of healing, even after all these years. She is still working to try to accept his death, so she can move on with her own life. I have often told her it is time to accept the reality and do something positive with her life. This is one situation where family is not able to help and professional help would be beneficial; however, only Laurie can make the choice she wants to move on.

# Jeanette's Story

I've heard it said, "God replaces one life with another," and so, that was how I *first* faced my journey through the loss of my brother Gary from a fatal car crash in 1981.

It was the start of Labor Day weekend—a time when I should have been experiencing one of the happiest moments of my life. My husband and I had just found out that week that we were expecting our first child. We had taken our parents out to dinner to tell them the happy news. When we dropped off my parents I was excited to tell my siblings, but only my sisters were home. My brother had been out for the evening. We proceeded home to drop off my in-laws, when I saw a dead animal on the side of the road. I remember saying, "Isn't it weird–God replaces one life with another." Well, that couldn't have rung more true when, the next morning, we were awakened early to the awful, heartbreaking news that my 28-year-old brother was killed in a single-car accident during the night.

What was, just hours ago, a feeling of utter euphoria, had now turned to despair. I remember everyone being concerned about me because I was pregnant. Family and friends were telling me not to "cry," to "calm down," and "take care of myself." Well, I've *never* been one to hold in any emotions or feelings. I'm certain that that's what has gotten me through many of life's "punches." "Let it out"—that's my philosophy–and so I did. I thought I'd never stop crying or feeling so incredibly sad and empty. Reflecting on this, I know that along with the support and prayers of family and friends, and a strong spiritual base, there were two very important factors that helped me embrace the pain of our loss…celebrate his life and move forward without my brother.

The first, of course, was our child I was carrying. The second was an unexpected time alone with my brother the week before he died. I had not had that kind of time with him in a long time. My family and I had just moved my younger sister into her dorm room at college and I said I would ride home with Gary in his car. In that 45-minute drive back home, we caught up on so much going on in our lives and I hinted I was pregnant. Although it saddens me he wasn't present in our daughter's lives, I thank God for that private time I had with him.

As much joy as the birth of our daughter (another daughter 3 years later and nieces and nephews over the years) brought into all our lives, I came to realize God never replaces one life with another. People and events in your life can fill a void, but your lost loved one remains in your heart. We are blessed with the extraordinary gift of "memory" and those memories have kept my brother alive in all our hearts.

~~~~~~

Laura and Jeanette are my two older sisters. You can see by reading my story and reading theirs that even though we are all sisters and had the same network of support, we all handled the situation differently. This shows once again how individual coping with death is. Everyone is an individual and handles things in their own way.

## *Nora's Story*

Here is a story is so hard to believe, but is all too real. Here is a normal family living their lives not knowing one would soon be gone. How often do we say to our siblings, "I can't now, but I'll meet up with you later." Maybe too often. We can never know what someone has on their minds, and even if we do, it doesn't mean we would be able to stop them from hurting themselves or even committing suicide. If we could, there wouldn't be such a thing as suicides or accidents. Nora's story shows just how deeply we are affected by a sibling's death. Not everyone can accept a death and move on quite as effectively as others. It shows just how individualized grieving and coping are.

## Nora's Story…

My brother, Steven committed suicide in 1982 at the age of 24. He was one year younger than me, and the youngest of four children. My oldest brother Ray was 28 at the time, followed by Edward age 27 and I was 25.

My family adored Steven. We did not know he was depressed. We did know he was having some difficulty starting a new job. Steven had dyslexia long before anyone knew what it was. There wasn't a name for dyslexia when Steven was growing up. He had started to train as an accountant and the dyslexia made it profoundly difficult. He had a girlfriend who he wanted to marry. She had broken up with him 4 years earlier. We thought he had gotten over her. Steven was discovered at a motel having shot himself in the head with pictures of his girlfriend surrounding him on the bed. It was through those prom pictures that Steven was identified.

His death forever altered my life and that of my family's. Steven called my brother Ray shortly before he left for the motel. He said to Ray, "I need to talk." Ray said, "Is it important or can it wait because I am in the middle of polyurethaning my floors." Steven replied, "It can and left for the motel." Raymond was never the same after Steven's death. Raymond evidently was predisposed to being bipolar and went into a major depressive episode. He blamed himself. Raymond never really recovered from Steven's death. Ray was two courses shy of finishing his doctorate in Psychological Research at Columbia—he never completed it. He gave up his apartment, became homeless for a while before eventually resurfacing. Raymond has not held down a job since. He helps to care for my mom now. My brother Edward has autism and for many years afterwards, heard Steven in the apartment they shared. My parents gave up on their retirement plans. My parents retired when Steven and I were still in high school. They bought the home of their dreams in Montauk Point on Long Island. They sold the house shortly after Steven's death and moved back to the apartment in NYC Steven shared with Edward. The joy went out of them and they had difficulty enjoying life. My father, who was a harsh disciplinarian, blamed himself profoundly. He worked to make up for any harm he had caused his children for the remainder of his life. My mother, who is 87 years old at this point, found satisfaction in volunteering her time at a senior citizen center and caring for my brother Edward. She has been unable to separate from her remaining sons since my father's death 3 years ago.

Suicide, losing someone to suicide has made all of us cling to each other extra tightly. I call my mother every morning to check on her and share the events of the previous day. I was married 3 years when my brother died. I cannot remember the evening of my brother's death no matter how hard I've tried. Was I home? Did he try to call me? I was in the field of Human Services at the time of his death and eventually went on to become a social worker. Since Steven's death, I have never been able to work with suicidal clients. I instead went into the field of community organization and program development. About 2 years after Steven's death, I started a Suicide Survivors group that ran for approximately 4 years. It was very helpful in terms of healing. There is such an incredible stigma around a suicidal death. Families are often blamed. We are too cold or overly enmeshed. Why are families who lose someone to cancer not blamed as we are? I met many caring, loving families who had experienced the same trauma that I did. It has been a very rough road for me. It cut short my carefree vision of the world. Before my brother's death, I felt there were many things in life that would not happen to me. I could no longer hide in that fallacy. I felt very vulnerable. Here it is 27 years later and this is what I have learned. We come up with explanations of why it happened that we could live with. We are not to blame.

If we could control others, our loved ones would still be alive.

We need to talk, at nauseam to people who understand and will not judge. I thank God every day my husband hung in there with me through it all.

There is much we do not understand about how our brains work and we are still in the dark ages when it comes to treating depression.

Not all suicides can be prevented.

It is shocking and can drop people to their knees for a very long time.

This loss made me a better parent.

I am vigilant when it comes to my children, but aware the same thing could occur and could be beyond my control.

Some people pass through our lives very quickly and maybe, just maybe they finished what they came here to do before us.

People commit suicide to escape incredible pain and misery. They are not looking to die, but looking to escape the pain.

Blaming others does not help. Always remember there are people who have a much worse life, who do not kill themselves.

Forgiving oneself is very hard. Talking to others in a similar place can help.

It is important to keep living.

Depression can run in families. I struggled with depression in my late teens, my father was depressed all of his life, until he was diagnosed with Parkinson's disease and given Sinemet. My oldest brother Ray is bipolar. My mother's grandfather committed suicide as well (we never knew about this until after Steven died). I suspect my mother also struggles with depression. My brother Edward has autism and struggles with depression. I believe there is a genetic component to depression for some people.

Medication does not help everyone.

It does alter one's life, but does not mean our lives need to be over. It is like a scar. Scars don't go away, they change who we are, but a scar doesn't end a life or ruin a life, unless we let it. Accepting our lives are forever altered can help. Stop trying to get your old life back...it is gone. Create a new one.

The pain becomes less as time goes on. In the beginning, I felt someone had ripped out my guts. I healed with the help of others who had traveled the same path and so can you.

I felt guilty aging at first, I was growing up and he would be 24 forever. I thought I was growing away from him. I thought it was my payback for a past life.

It can screw with our family placement. I am now the youngest of four siblings. It was not supposed to be that way.

Insensitive remarks come from ignorance, much the same as racist remarks. They hurt a lot, but instead of suffering in silence, I use the opportunity to educate others now.

If your sibling was your favorite, it is not always possible to achieve that closeness with another sibling, no matter how much we want it. No one really replaces another.

You and your sibling may view the death and its causes differently. Allow each other to grieve differently.

I am very grateful I had my brother Steven to grow up with. I still miss him, but know I will see him again someday. Never give up on celebrating your loved one's life. The method of death does not detract from the life they led or detract from the worth of their life, regardless of what others may say. Families can survive this.

~~~~~~

When I received Nora's story, it brought tears to my eyes for everything they went through, but at the same time, I felt such an inspiration, hope and sense of courage and strength. I know how difficult it is to go through losing someone due to an accident. You don't get to say your goodbyes or last words, but to me, going through loss due to a suicide seems much harder, because of the things Nora listed. Families do tend to be blamed for not seeing any signs. Signs may not be visible to anyone. Families are not to blame! Reading what Nora's family went through and to see she was still able, with help from others, to move her life forward and help others going through the same difficult process is wonderful. I think this is such an amazing way to heal, and in the same token, help others to heal.

Here is yet another story that shows proof life can and will go on, only if you let it. Let others in to help you. Start doing something proactive to help others. It will help you immensely, just as well as help others. Learn something from the tragedy and do something positive with it.

*Stories of Hope and Inspiration*

# *Tracey's Story*

Here is another heartbreaking story of suicide. It shows how some of us can be so heartbroken over a relationship that we feel we can no longer go on with our lives. However, it also shows how a sibling can turn a tragedy into something positive to help others by what was learned.

**Tracey's Story…**

My name is Tracey Sherman and I lost my beautiful brother Rick to suicide in November 2004. Rick was 39-years-old and I was 33-years-old. My brother was the most easy going, down to earth, peace-loving and kind-hearted person. Unfortunately, he saw his depression as a sign of weakness and chose to hide the severity of it from his family and friends. Although we were aware, he was feeling down from a breakup with a girlfriend, we had no idea he was suicidal.

The suicide completely turned my life and the lives of my family members completely upside down and inside out. We were angry, shocked, grief stricken and confused. We spent a good deal of time trying to put the pieces of the puzzle together to try to understand how this could happen to our "normal" family. Our lives were scarred and we were now considered "survivors." I spent a lot of time in therapy, support groups and reading about depression and suicide. I needed to understand how this could happen before I was willing to accept what had happened. It was a long process of being completely consumed with the loss and the pain around it. I talked about the loss a lot and this helped me tremendously because it was already on my mind 24/7. I definitely felt denial played a role in the early stages of the loss. I also know I had an inability to sit still for long periods of time. I had to keep moving and going nonstop.

Three years after the loss, I began working as an administrative assistant for The American Foundation for Suicide Prevention. I then moved onto a job that I am very proud of. I am a social worker providing counseling for suicide survivors and running a support group for them as well. I know I have been helpful to these survivors during a very dark and difficult period of their lives.

I feel talking about the loss is critical to the healing process. Losing a sibling is so painful and it helps to release the pain by talking, crying and memorializing him/her. I also found a support group very helpful because it enabled me to see I was not alone in what I was experiencing.

~~~~~

Here is another story that shows how you can learn something positive and turn something so very tragic into something you can learn and give back to help others. Tracey and her family tried to put the "pieces of the puzzle together," but that often is impossible to do to find the answers. She turned her situation into something positive to help others.

# *WyKisha's Story*

Here is yet another heart-wrenching story of suicide. However, again, it also shows how such a tragedy can turn into something positive to help others.

### WyKisha's Story... "I've Survived 5"

February 6, 2004, the day Johnny died. That date is etched in my brain for all eternity. On that day, a voice on the other end of my phone told me my brother had died by suicide. If someone would have told me then I would be speaking to a group of people about surviving a suicide loss, I would have thought they were crazy. I would have said, "How can I talk to someone about surviving a suicide, when it's killing me!" Nonetheless, here I am, sharing my story and healing from my loss. I've been riding this emotional roller coaster for 5 years and I'm still here, still healing, still living. I've survived 5!

In these past 5 years, I struggled with trying to figure out what's supposed to be "normal" for me now. What's appropriate for me now that I'm a Survivor of Suicide? I remember thinking, "I just need someone to tell me I'm going to be okay." So, I'm here to tell you all today what I wanted so desperately for someone to tell me then…"You're going to be okay!"

**Everybody say…I'm Okay!**
**I'm okay with crying when I need to. (Everybody say…I'm Okay!)**

I firmly believe there are two ways you can deal with your grief and your pain, voluntarily or involuntarily. Those tears are going to come whether you like it or not. Therefore, you need to allow yourself time to shed the pain from your body.

On the other hand, it's not okay to hold the pain in until is festers into something that's not healthy for you. For the first year or two after my brother's death, I internalized a lot of my pain. I was afraid to upset my parents. I was afraid of scaring my son. I was worried about what people would think of me. I bottled all of that in and I started having problems with depression and anxiety. It wasn't until I started allowing myself to grieve that I began to heal.

**I'm okay with getting angry. (Everybody say…I'm Okay!)**
You're going to get mad; you're going to get pissed!

And that's okay! How many of you have thought to yourself, "I'm pissed you left me! I hate I'm hurting like this! Why did you do this?" I'm dealing with anger toward my brother right now. I'm angry he missed my wedding, my college graduation, the birth of my daughter and my son's first football season! I'm angry he left me here to take care of my parents by myself. He was the oldest. This was his job.

What's not okay is to feel guilty about it. Like crying, anger is a natural human reaction. I read in the "Survivor of Suicide

Handbook" that guilt is what we feel when we place our anger where it doesn't belong...on ourselves. I remember beating myself up so much for even thinking of being angry with Johnny, but now I'm okay with saying, "I love you, but I'm really pissed at you today."

**I'm okay with the "Why" question. (Everybody say...I'm Okay!)**

Wanting to understand your loss is normal. However, it's not okay to let it consume you. The cold fact is...the only person that can answer "why" is already gone. Maybe one day, there will come a time when you will find an answer that will bring you comfort or perhaps one day you will finally accept a satisfying explanation for your loss may not exist. Unfortunately, finding the answer to "why" won't bring them back to us. That's why it's important to let go of "why" so you can begin accepting your loss and healing. It wasn't until I was passed the urge to know "why" that I stopped beating myself up about what I would have, could have and should have done to prevent Johnny's suicide.

**I'm okay with talking about it. (Everybody say...I'm Okay!)**

You need to talk about it. The stigma of suicide can be so crippling for a survivor. It escalates those feelings of guilt and shame, and keeps you from reaching out for help. I stopped telling people Johnny died by suicide after I got funny looks and heard people say we must have had "family problems" for him to do something like that. I felt ashamed. I also felt defensive. I spent so much time defending my brother, my family and myself that I lost focus on healing.

Then I found the Survivor of Suicide groups, where I met people who had lost someone too, and I could talk about my loss without getting funny faces or insensitive questions. I could talk to people who had survived 5, 10, and 15 years after suicide. I finally found someone who told me, "You're going to be okay!"

**I'm okay with smiling again. (Everybody say...I'm Okay!)**

I know sometimes it's hard getting passed reliving the funeral and the day you found out about the death. I also know sometimes those fond memories of your loved ones can hurt more than help. There have been times where a familiar smell or a familiar song has brought me to my knees in sorrow. Johnny was a handsome guy and he knew it. When you asked him, "Johnny, how are you feeling today?" his response would always be "cute." I remember after Johnny died I ran into his best friend and I asked him, "Hey, how are you doing?" His response to me was "Cute," just like Johnny would have done. I tried to put on a smile, but I couldn't fight back the tears that came with the memory.

Now those memories comfort me. Those memories bring a smile to my face. One day, you will be able to smile again, too. You'll be able to relive those memories and laugh aloud again.

**It's okay to move on! (Everybody say...I'm Okay!)**

You won't forget them! They were very special to you. They are why you're here today. There's a part of me severely damaged by losing Johnny, but I'm healing and my life is still going on. I got into a very bad habit of blaming Johnny's death for everything going wrong in my life. Until one day, my best friend sat me down and asked me, "When are you going to stop using your brother's death as an excuse to stop living." As much as I hated to admit it at the time...she was right. I blamed myself for his decision, I felt guilty about moving on and I used that loss as an excuse to stay stuck in a pit of despair.

It's not okay to stop living.

I want to leave you with just a few final things, and then, I'm going to let you go so we can start the walk:

To Moms and Dads: you loved your baby and they knew that. Their death is not a reflection of your parenting. This was their personal decision.

To Sisters and Brothers: I connect more closely with you all because I know first-hand what it's like to lose a sibling. Although, we shared secrets with our brother or sister, this one secret they *CHOSE* to keep to themselves.

To Husbands, Wives and significant others: When you choose to spend your life with someone you may sometimes feel like you're responsible for them. When they ended their life, you may have felt you failed. Know you are not responsible for this death.

To Sons and Daughters: Please know your mom or dad's decision to die had nothing to do with you. I'm sure your parent loved you. They were in pain and didn't know how to live with it. Cling to the people closest to you for support and talk about it as much as you need to.

To friends and other family members: Although you lost someone very dear to you, look around, see a reflection of them in their families and don't be afraid to talk to them about your friend.

If you take nothing else away from me today, please remember *I'M OKAY*. Etch that in your heart, say it and believe it. **Say it with me, again…I'M OKAY!**

~~~~~~

WyKisha's story is so empowering to me. Here is someone who was able to stand in front of a crowd of people while still coping and helped everyone, and herself, say and feel, "I'M OKAY," and *BELIEVE IT!*

# CHAPTER NINE
# *What Would Help You Heal?*

What do you think would help you heal? Think about this. Get your pen or pencil and your notebook, and write down at the top of your paper, "What would help me heal?" Now, just start writing down whatever comes to mind. Don't think anything is stupid, silly or ridiculous. Just write everything down. Don't think about what you are writing. Give yourself about 15 minutes just to write these ideas down and when you have given it an honest 15 minutes, put down your pen.

Read every idea you wrote down. Think about each one and say it aloud. Pick out the top 5 that seem to be the best and would really help. (Put down as many ideas that are comfortable for you). If you come up with a lot of ideas, pick out your best 10 to 15 ideas and put them in order from best down. Now that you have your top ideas, write down the idea at the top of a sheet of paper. Now write down ways to expand on those ideas. Write down everything imaginable. Again, don't worry if it sounds dumb or silly. No one else needs to see this. This is just for you. I suggest doing an idea a day and then focus on doing what you have written down. This is to be a positive thing to help you; not negative, such as talking about my sibling once a day. Then you can expand it to work, such as, you will bring their name up in conversation and just mention something about them that made you happy. Things like that or I need to start exercising to make myself feel better. I will start walking for 15 minutes three times a week. You can be as creative as you like. Anything that will help you feel better is healthy and healing. It may even be you will start getting more involved with your religion or volunteering somewhere, changing your career or taking courses.

Think of ways you can change your life to get out of your depression, pain, or whatever it is you are feeling. Sometimes if we focus our attention on others and not ourselves, we feel better. When you start doing for others, you feel better. I'm not saying do for others so you ignore and forget your pain. I'm saying consider helping others to help you feel better and help you get over your pain, not forget it or repress it. It may help you realize exactly where some of your pain is centered.

As I have mentioned before, maybe you can learn more about what your sibling died of and help others who are going through the same thing, such as mental illness or a disease process. You hear of many parents and older siblings getting involved with pushing for laws to be passed about guns or fireworks. These people are doing something positive because of a tragedy. Look at Mothers Against Drunk Driving. That has become such a big organization. They are doing so much to help educate people on drunk driving and helping victim's families. I am not saying you need to go big; these are just examples of what people can do to change the pain into something good to help others.

There are so many things you can do to help and many organizations to help you find peace. You just need to think about it and write down what it is that would help you. You may need to get into a state of peace before doing this. You cannot have a terrible day and try to sit and write down ideas. I would suggest going into a quiet room and sit either on a chair or sit crossed-leg and meditate. Meditate on the thought of, "What will help you heal?" Focus on this first. You need to be quiet and peaceful. You can do this, even if it is for just a few short moments. You need is enough time to quiet your mind so all you are thinking about is healing and what would help you get there. Then you can sit and write down every idea that comes into your mind. Don't cross out any idea, even if they sound way out there. Keep every idea and eventually go through each and every idea. As I explained before, expand on each idea. Ask yourself questions about each idea. What do I mean by this? Think about each question and write down answers. You will find you can come up with very good ways to help you move on and heal. It just takes time and commitment. Get a coach to help you be accountable and assist you if you need help staying focused on your goals. It is not always an easy process to do on your own. If you are having a hard time doing this, make it one of your goals to accomplish. Make it a commitment. You can even write up a contract and have someone witness and date it. When you are accountable to someone else, you seem to be more apt to work on it, such as with a life coach. I have worked with Jack Canfield's coaches to get more experience, and it does help when you are accountable. You feel like you really have to push to reach your goals. You can even make short-term goals out of it; for example, "I will work on one idea a week." Each day of the week, I will expand on this idea. You need to make it interesting for yourself. When you are depressed and don't want to move on, you need something to really get you motivated. Make it fun. You do need some fun in your life.

Surround yourself with happiness. Make a collage of all your happy, fun times, with and/or without your sibling. Put pictures of silly things you have done with your friends that make you happy and laugh. Write things on there that were only good memories. Take a yoga class. Play happy, upbeat music. Go for a walk every morning and think about good things. Get an MP3 player or CD and listen to motivational talks. Make a set date with some of your friends to have a night to do something fun; maybe watch a funny movie and eat popcorn. Whatever you can think of that is fun and silly for you. Do things to get you pumped and moving in the right direction. Just throw yourself into the positive things. Don't fake it. Deal with the issues at hand, but with the added positive and happy thoughts coming in, it will be easier to deal with the negatives, and deal with them more objectively and with a clearer, more peaceful mind.

There is no going back; you need to deal with what you are dealt. Here are some ideas I hope you have gotten from this: Forgive yourself. Do something nice for yourself. Take a hot bubble bath, relax and take care of yourself. Go exercise. Exercise is a great way to deal with stress. Don't forget your sibling; talk about them. Think about them and talk to them. Write in a journal. I have seen some people make memoir books of their loved ones. There are beautiful things you can do to honor your sibling. Be creative. Use the negative energy you have and do something positive with it; a tribute to your loved one everyone may enjoy. Ask your sibling to help guide you through those rough times. Remember, they wouldn't want you to stop living. Don't feel guilty for living your life, smiling and having fun.

Many things I do that make me think, "Gary would have been so proud of me for this one!" I often think when I'm doing something he taught me, he is watching over me and laughing, saying, "Way to go Peewee!" It makes me proud I can do these things and have bettered my life because of him. I have been able to do this because I have grieved him and have moved on. Write down all the positive things in your life because of your sibling and things they have taught you, and say a prayer thanking them for enriching your life so much.

Also, please remember grieving, coping and moving on do not mean you can't cry and that you need to forget them. I have grieved Gary's loss, accepted he is not coming back, but believe his spirit still lives on, and I am living my life to the fullest; in a way, he would be very proud of, and still occasionally cry. If this is difficult for you, then think of it this way…live your life if not for yourself, but in their honor. Do it for them, then gradually you may realize you are really doing it for yourself. This is a good thing.

In the next section of this book, "Moving On," we will be moving towards the next step, expanding on where you are right now, and how it feels and what moving on means to you. I will be focusing on more of the things you can be doing now to push yourself forward in your own life. What humps have you gotten over you are proud of? Where are you now with your life, not just with coping, but how you have coped and moved your life towards reaching your goals. Do you have goals written down? If not, we will go through goal writing and setting limits for yourself. Also, what will it take to move forward and what changes do you still need to make to be able to move forward and on with your life if you have not yet gotten to that point.

At the end of the book you will see the workbook with activities to do to help you stay on track with moving on. This will help to stay focused and following it will make you feel you need to do what you write in it. You will feel more accountable when you have written it down or, again, get a coach who can help you be more accountable to stay on track. Each week you are accountable for what you wrote down that you would commit to do for the week.

Congratulate yourself on finishing this first book in the series. You have taken that first step to healing and moving on. You need to appreciate yourself, forgive yourself if you have guilt, appreciate your sibling for being a part of your life and giving a part of themselves to you, and then start working on your life. Be Grateful! Continue to love your sibling and celebrate their life! You don't need to forget them, just don't stop living your life. Live your life to the fullest in their honor. Work on the items I have listed in this book and get professional help if you need. I also am a life coach. You can e-mail me at lifeguidanceandsolutions@gmail.com or robertastackcostantino@gmail.com to have a consultation or to share your story of a loss. You can move on, live your life to the fullest, and yes, even fulfill your dreams! So, start now! It is time for "MOVING ON."

# Part Two
# *"Moving On"*

## INTRODUCTION

*I*n the first part of the book, "I Miss You, Gary," I gave you my story and stories from other people who had gone through the loss of a sibling from various circumstances. I gave some ideas on how to cope and grieve. In this second part, "Moving On," I will be giving you ways in which to "Move On" with your life. I work in the field of Occupational Therapy and am a Life Coach, Motivational Speaker, and in the process of becoming certified in Grief Counseling. This book is set up somewhat like a coaching session, with each part moving onto the next phase to reaching your goals. The goal of this series is to be able to move on and live a happy and productive life after losing a sibling.

In the first part, I told you about dealing with my brother Gary's accident and death, coping and grieving strategies, and sibling rivalry. I purposely added stories from others who have gone through a sibling's death, to give hope and inspiration to those of you who feel you can't go on and are looking for help.

In this part, "Moving On," I will discuss how to move on with your life, your career, and being *YOU*. I will also talk about what it will take to get you to move on to the next phase of your life and what changes you need to make in order to get over your loss and move on.

## CHAPTER TEN
# *Moving On*

*I*t is amazing how life works and how those we love always seem to take care of us, even when they are not physically with us anymore. When we're not sure what to do at some point in our lives, some "coincidence" happens to make the decision for us. This happened several years after Gary's death, however, when I saw Gary's friend years earlier in my healing process and I felt the same way. I went to pick up my daughter who was helping my dad take carryout orders at a church fish fry (before he passed away). I went inside and there is my brother Gary's best friend's sister who I haven't seen for years. We said "Hi" and talked for a while. When I turned, there he was, Gary's best friend. I didn't run, but quickly walked over after we both turned at the same time and saw each other. I gave him the biggest hug and started to cry. They weren't sad tears, not in anyway. My sister and I had just been talking about him and here he was, right in front of me. He looked older than the last time I saw him and I could have sworn I saw Gary standing right next to him. I almost had to laugh because I was picturing how Gary would look at 55. I told his friend about what all I have been doing. We talked for a while and said our good-byes. When I walked away, I felt good. I cried, but they were happy tears. Seeing his friend brought back such happy memories of Gary, growing up, and it just made me happy.

Just because I cried, doesn't mean I haven't coped with Gary's death and his being gone. It is definitely okay to cry. If I would have said, "Why is he alive and Gary isn't, that's not fair, I can't stand to look at him or be around him," then I would have a problem. However, I was able to look at one of my brother's best friends whom I haven't seen in probably 10 to 15 plus years, be happy and bring happy memories to the forefront of my mind. That is a wonderful feeling. This shows I can be around situations that dealt with Gary's life, move into life without Gary and be okay. As I said, I also saw the same friend a couple years after Gary died and I was still happy to see him then. It showed me then I had moved on, but this story seemed appropriate, even though it was many years after Gary's death. This shows I had coped and moved on. I felt it was normal to cry when I saw Gary's friend. It was great to see him after all these years, plus, I was just talking about him and had been worrying how I was going to start this part of the book. Then, "Bam," right in front of my face, there he is. Just as I mentioned in, I Miss You Gary, Gary usually really has to put something out right in front of me to say, "Hello, here it is. Use this for your book!" So, thank you Gary, once again for helping me out!

I think at Gary's wake and funeral, I had feelings of why did it have to be Gary, why couldn't it have been one of his friends, or someone else instead. It was very hard to see his friends then. I was angry they were here and Gary wasn't. It wasn't fair. This isn't how you feel when you move on. This is how you feel when your sibling first dies and you have not yet accepted and grieved your loss. You will notice when you see a sibling's friend or co-worker, it should get easier for you and the feelings of anger and/or jealousy dissipate. As you notice your feelings changing more positively then you know you are on the road to healing and moving on. I think the biggest clue to me I was coping and moving on was when I was able to talk about Gary without a tight chest and feeling as if someone was stabbing me in the heart, and when I could talk about him and not cry. Then I was able to see his friends and be happy to see them, rather than jealous they were alive and he wasn't.

There is no timeline for moving on. However, if it is several years and you still cannot go on with your plans and move on...then there is a block in allowing you to progress forward. Personally, I had a very hard time when Gary died. It was so unexpected, but I was able to move on. I had an occasional setback once in a while, but that is normal. You always have moments, such as birthdays and special occasions; you get upset, sad and really want them back. I want Gary back every single day. The difference is I can miss him and talk to him, but I am realistic and know he cannot come back and I can't just die along with him. I need to have a life, a career, fun and enjoy life. There has already been one death, why make it two. What good does that really do? If you truly are unable to move on and you don't know why you can't, maybe it is time to go talk with someone and get down to the real issue at hand as to why you can't go on with your life. Is it guilt? Is it fear? Maybe you need to ask your sibling permission to move on. Did something happen in your childhood you are suppressing? There can be a number of issues going on that you really don't understand or have a clue about. This is where talking with someone objective can help you get over the hump. Consider it.

Think for a moment. I mean really think. What good does it really do for you to just stay stagnant and not progress forward? Are there any positives to that? I don't think you will find any. Just because you feel better when you feel guilty, doesn't mean you should be miserable. That doesn't make any sense. Again, as I have said in the first part, it is time to get over it and move on. That doesn't mean you are disrespecting your sibling, but the contrary; you are disrespecting them by not living your life. It is your choice. Talk to them. Write to them. Write a journal and tell them what you are feeling. Figure out what the problem is. As I mentioned before, you may come up with some questions or answers you did not know even existed.

Think for a while on what exactly "Moving On" means to you, personally. I will tell you what it means to me, by going on with your life and moving forward, and living your life to the fullest; however, "Moving On" may not mean that to you. Again, everyone is an individual and it may mean something different to you. When you are done thinking about this, write down what it means to YOU!

After you have given this some time, wrote down what "Moving On" means to you and have edited it to really know what it means, think of things you can do to help you reach this. What can you write down as long-term goals and short-term goals to help you move on? This is where the goal writing can help you out. You need to make this a goal-oriented process to help you. Write down the short-term and long-term goals and 3 to 5 daily tasks to do to help you reach them. Once again, this will help you to stay on track with getting to where you're aiming. If you think about it but don't write it down, it is less likely you will take action. Even by just writing down the goals, you may still not take action, but it has been shown when you write goals, you are more accountable to them and to yourself to achieve them. This is where the daily 3-5 action steps will keep you more accountable.

I want you to write down what you have done to move on in your terms. Really think about this and be honest, come on; do it. What has helped you to move on *AND* what has held you back? Now look at what has helped and think about other things that you could do to help you to move on. Write down at least 3 to 5 items for now. What could you really do to push you forward? Don't just write down the easy things. Really, think down deep and write down those difficult things that aren't that easy to deal with. Don't push the hard ones aside. Write them down. Now, go to the items that have held you back. Think about why and how they have held you back. Write down your feelings and then write down how you can change those feelings. What can you do to turn those into ways to help you move forward?

This may sound difficult and redundant, but it helps. The idea is to help you really think about this. Dig deep down into your soul, into all the thoughts you have been pushing aside that you don't want to deal with. Those ones you want to push up to the surface and deal with. Just like anything else, you need to deal with those demons and all those thoughts that keep pushing you deeper and deeper into a "state of being stuck in limbo." If you find this too difficult, check into talking with someone about it. If a family member, religious leader or a friend is not able to help, go seek out a professional. There might be something there you cannot deal with yourself. Know your limits of how much you can do on your own or with just family or friends. Be honest with yourself if you need professional help. There is nothing wrong with seeking out a counselor or other professional. You will thank yourself later on.

Part of the moving on process entails dealing with life events your sibling cannot partake in and enjoy with you. Believe me...this can be very difficult. On the day of my wedding, I forced myself not to think of him. I stood at the altar knowing I was in this same place with my brother at his funeral mass. It is hard to put that out of your head, even though it was 9 years after his accident, it felt like yesterday. I knew if I started thinking about him I would break down and that would be it. So, I thought of the honeymoon and the food at the reception, to keep me occupied. I made it all the way through the whole wedding mass without a tear.

Another difficult time was when I had my two girls. He would have spoiled all his nieces and nephews like crazy. They know all about him, though. Even when they were babies, I would tell them about their Uncle Gary. My little one is like him, somewhat. She takes after me when I was little and is a worker. She would help my dad outside cutting grass or whatever needed doing. Gary would have loved having her around, teaching her things, like he taught me, and I think about how they would have gotten along. Both my girls have some of his qualities and he would have loved that.

My father died on November 6, 2009, and was buried on his 81$^{st}$ birthday, right next to Gary. It was difficult going through that thinking Gary should be here. He was the oldest. He should be helping us and taking charge. However, he wasn't there and it was us three girls, taking care of everything and taking care of our mom, who has dementia and has gone downhill quickly since my dad's passing. There are times when I think about the emptiness in our lives now my dad and Gary both are gone. Then I think about all I have learned from them and how they have taught me to be the person I am meant to be, and I am living to be. I am so grateful to both of them. I was very close to both of them and had the same type of relationship with both of them. I don't get angry Gary isn't here. He can't be. It is just a fact. I wish he were. It sure would make things much easier for us, but, we are persevering and we are doing a great job I think both my dad and Gary would be proud of.

These life-changing events can be and are difficult, but it is just another area of life you need to overcome and pursue on with your life endeavors. You do what needs to be done, also, take care of yourself, most importantly, and heal and then move on. Don't numb yourself to these life events. Learn from them what you can so you can grow and become the person you are meant to be. Each loss is for you to grow from, if you just let yourself.

Again, just with grieving and coping with your loss, you have to talk, talk and talk about your pain, about your fears, your loss and moving on. Discuss with your family and friends you miss your sibling during the important times in your life. Don't hold those thoughts in. Discuss them. Think about what they would have said to you, how they would have been very happy for you and use that to help you be happy with your exciting life events, and be happy in their honor.

As you go through your daily activities, keep in mind how you can do something differently to help you move on. Surrounding yourself with things that you love to do and are absolutely passionate about helps. The more you focus on positive aspects…the easier and happier you can and will be. You want to have quality in your life. You want to have the best life ever. Don't you? You only get one chance, so make it the best.

# CHAPTER ELEVEN
# *Where Are You Now?*

Where are you right this moment in the coping process? Are you able to think about your sibling without crying? Can you talk about your sibling without having a tight chest and sobbing? Are you able to say the words "My sibling is dead?" You need to think about how you react and act when you think and talk about your sibling. Are you afraid of talking about them? Do you think people won't care? Do you care if people care? Personally, I never really thought about or cared if it bothered people if I spoke about my brother. I don't mean that in a rude way, but it was so important for me to talk about him because I felt better when I did. I didn't want anyone to forget him. I think it made me feel close to him and memorialize him.

Take your time with this. In what ways, have you coped? In what ways, have you moved on? If you haven't, why? How long has your sibling been gone? Remember, everyone heals in their own due time, however, if it is 3+ years and you have not moved on at all, you need to think about why you haven't. Are you holding yourself back? Do you feel others are holding you back and making you feel guilty for trying to move on?

Are you being your own worst enemy? Have you ever heard of the term "self-talk?" Self-talk is when you talk negatively (or positively) to yourself. Things like, "I can't do this." "I can't go on without them." "I just want to die." "I would be better off gone." Are you guilty of this? I would have to say you probably are if it has been a couple of years, or so, and you still cannot cope with your sibling's death.

This is not impossible to get over. Many people do this every single day. Who hasn't? The difference is if you are literally stuck in negative self-talk or you just do it occasionally, and then talk yourself back out of it with positive self-talk. Honestly, I have done it, too. However, when I do, I usually get out of it with positive self-talk pretty quickly. In a really bad situation, like with my dad's death and dealing with my mom's dementia, it would sometimes take me a day or two to get a good night's sleep, and then, I would wake up in the morning with a totally different perspective. I do not keep negatively self-talking to myself.

You can see how you can change the self-talk. You simply change your negative self-talk into positive self-talk. I know, I said, "Simply." We all know it is not that easy. It is not a simple task to "simply" turn the negative into a positive. You have to believe you can and you have to believe in yourself. You don't necessarily have to believe the self-talk initially, but if you keep saying and thinking it, you eventually do believe it and start thinking more positively.

Some ways to do this are to keep saying the positive. For example, "I will have a happy day and will do something fun today." Then, keep repeating this and actually try to do something fun. Another thing you can do is to make a slide show on your computer of happy and fun things. Things that make you laugh. This can include your sibling or not. That is up to you. Surround yourself with funny things. Make a poster of funny and happy things. Buy yourself some flowers to smell. Call a friend and go see a funny movie, or have funny movie night at home. These are just a few examples. Be creative. By just repeating the positive, even though you may not believe it, the more you repeat it, the more your mind will believe it. The mind is a very amazing and powerful tool. It will make happen what you think and believe. Go watch "The Secret" movie or read the book. This is definitely a positive self-talk inspiration for you. So, go on; do something fun and positive…right now!

Where are you right now in your personal life because of your sibling's loss? Have you become closer to your family and friends? Have you alienated family and friends? How do you feel about yourself? These deep questions you need to think about and write down the answers to, honestly. It doesn't help if you just brush the surface of your feelings and say, "Oh, I am okay. Sure, I miss them, but I am doing okay." when in reality, you have lost your sense of self and who you really are. You can't say, "I am okay." when you have lost your friends, alienated your family or don't discuss your sibling at all, for fear you will totally break down and not be able to function at all.

So, again, think about it. Where are you right now? Have you begun to live this new and different life without your sibling? Have you made any changes to your life? Positive ones? Negative ones? I hope that the negative thoughts and lifestyle are gone, and you are dealing with positive changes. You now have to learn how to live this new life without your sibling. Think of it as new and different, not negative and lonesome. It is a new, different life that you need to make the necessary adaptations to be happy and grow.

Remember what I told you in the first section of the book, how with each loss in your life, be it loss of a job, a divorce, loss of independence, whatever, you will become the person you are meant to be if you only use these experiences to grow from. You really need to think about what you are meant to learn from each experience. What has the person taught you in life? What have you learned from their death? What has the whole situation taught you? You need to figure out, learn and grow from it. Everything happens for a reason. It is just looking past the pain to realize what you can learn from it. This isn't always an easy thing to do. When you are in pain it is difficult to say, "Hey, what can I learn from this?" You need to. This will help you grow as a person and help you to become who you are meant to be. This is not an immediate response. This is something you can do once you have accepted the situation.

In this section, hopefully you have gone through your grieving and are coping with your sibling's death, and are moving on with your life, career, living your life and learning who this different *YOU* is in this different life. You will have occasional setbacks. This is a normal part of life. However, it is how you deal with them that is key. If you accept the setbacks as a normal part of life and deal with them and move on, this is not a problem. The problem lies in if you have a setback and just go back into grieving and/or bad habits.

This is when setbacks become issues. Don't panic when you have a meltdown. Work yourself through it, realize it is okay and learn from it.

When you get to this point of being able to move on, my hope is you have been able to move on, not only with your grief, but with your life overall. My hope is you have started rebuilding your new life...your life without your sibling. It doesn't mean it has to be a bad life, just a different life. It can and should be a good life. Go back to the first section where I explained about writing goals. Always have goals. When you have reached a goal, write a new goal. As you move on, write new ones to help push you forward. Write them for all aspects of your life. Make sure you don't get into the habit of just writing goals and not working towards reaching them. Remember to write down your long-term and short-term goals and each day write down 3-5 items you can do to help you achieve them. I do this every day. I have my long and short-term goals, but I also make weekly and daily goals. This way it really pushes me to get things done. With my hectic lifestyle, I need reminders, otherwise; I will honestly forget what I wanted to do. This way, if I have everything written down right in front of me, I have no excuse. I do have to admit I don't always get every item done on my list. If I had an extra 3-5 hours a day, then I guarantee I would get everything done. We all have hectic lifestyles with jobs, kids and other responsibilities; it is not always possible to get everything done. Don't hate yourself or punish yourself when you don't get everything done. Push it to the next day. That is okay. Everyone is human. As long as you get it done in an allotted period of time, hey, you're fine. Don't put extra pressure on yourself at this time that you don't need. This isn't going to help you move on. Push yourself, but be reasonable. In this phase of your life, the last thing you want to do is to put extra pressure and stress on yourself. The idea of the goals is to make life less stressful. Make sure you are giving them an honest effort. Do not dismiss every item every day because you lack the motivation. If you are not motivated, then make that one of your goals to get yourself motivated!

Another proactive step you can take is to join a support group; either one on the internet or go to a formal support group, where you can be face to face with others going through similar situations and understand what you are going through. This is a good support system for you. Many times people meet new friends at these groups, connect outside of the meeting times, and continue to help each other as friends. A professionally trained individual, such as a psychologist, psychiatrist and counselor, or an individual who has gone through the process of grieving and wants to help others learn how to cope, grieve and move on.

There are different kinds of support groups. Some are more intimate, you can discuss openly in a small group, and others are less intimate, and are larger groups where you are educated on coping/ grieving. You need to see which best fits your personal needs. Do you want not to be seen, asked questions and asked to participate? Then I suggest going to a larger group. If you prefer to share your story with others, go to a small group. If you don't want to leave your house, there is the internet. Many wonderful support groups online have chat rooms and message boards to write what you are feeling, and a group leader will write back to you, or someone else in the group. It is a wonderful way to see others are going through the same thing you are and many are at the same stage as you are in your healing process. There is someone at every stage of healing in these groups. You are bound to connect with someone.

How has your life changed since you have begun to move on? I asked this earlier, but let's go more in depth now. How have your thoughts and beliefs changed since you accepted your sibling's death? In being able to move on, you had to accept their loss. So, after accepting their loss, how have you changed? Are you a stronger person? Are you more patient of others' and yourself? How are you different? What have you changed in your life? Are you writing goals for yourself? Give these questions some deep thought. This does not mean you are forgetting your sibling, it means you are living.

Where are you in your career; be it a homemaker or working outside the home? Have you been able to do your job emotionally and physically? Have you been happy in your job? Do you have too much stress right now or not enough work to keep you working towards your goals? Have you made your short-term and long-term career goals? If you have not been happy with your job since your loss, it may not be the job at all. It may be you are stuck in grief and not coping or maybe you just need something more now. Look at your job and your career goals after writing them down. Do they match with each other? If your job is not leading you toward your goals, you need to start looking at how you can reach those goals. Do you need to take some courses? Do you need to change positions at your job or change how you do your job? Do you want to make a total career change or just a positional change? Are you looking at changing your career because of your sibling's death and going into counseling, the medical field, etc.? Where are you right now?

It is important for you to see how far you have come in the healing process. You will still have down times, but when you do, they may not be as often, and they may not be quite as difficult. When you do have your down times, you can think about the good times you had with your sibling and realize you can live a happy and productive life without them because you will always have them in your heart. Be proud of yourself of how far you have come. You *ARE* moving on.

If you are not at the point of moving on yet and accepting of your sibling's death, consider a support group, if family and friends are not doing the trick for you. This is a good first-step towards getting help. If your sibling just passed away, that is a different story. You need to give yourself time to grieve, accept and get to the point of moving on. This is for those of you who have lost their sibling a couple years ago and aren't moving forward. However, you can use these guidelines to help you in your healing process. Don't force yourself to move on before you are ready, though. You need time to go through your individual healing process. It takes time.

For those of you who have lost multiple siblings, it probably will take you longer to move on after each sibling. I lost one brother. I can't imagine losing more than one sibling, especially in a short period of time. I am a support group leader on an internet web site and I get people writing me that have lost multiple siblings within months, then a spouse and/or parent. My heart goes out to all of you. It is so difficult to lose someone, but two, three, or more, I could not even imagine going through that. Some say with each sibling lost, it gets more difficult for each. I have had some people say it was not like that for them. That it was more difficult for the ones they were closer to. Again, it is very individual. Allow yourself more time to heal in these multiple losses and definitely think about seeking out a counselor. A counselor can help you through this most difficult process to live your life. This situation will take much more time, so allow yourself that time.

I hope that in this section, you have been able to assess where you are in moving forward. I have given you ideas to assist you in finding where you are in this process, not only personally, but also in your career. If you are not happy with any area of your life, you need to assess why or have a counselor assess why. You may not be able to go it alone if you are stuck in every area of your life. Writing your goals and your dreams down will allow you to see where you want to be. After doing that, you need to figure out how by setting short-term goals to reach those dreams. You can start with a "bucket list." This is a list of everything you want to do before you die. It can be anything you want to accomplish, even silly-sounding things. Nobody else needs to see it. You can write down 50 to 100 things down. This sounds like a lot, but as you get started, you just start thinking of things you want to do, people you want to meet, places you want to go, foods you want to eat, etc. Try it. It really is fun to do and helps you see where you want to go.

If you truly try some or all of these things, you really will see changes in your life. According to Marshall Goldsmith in his book, "MOJO: How to Get It, How to Keep It, How to Get It Back If You Lose It" he says, "Very few people achieve positive, lasting change without ongoing follow-up. Unless they know at the end of the day (or week or month) that someone is going to measure, if they're doing what they promised to do, most people fall prey to inertia. They continue to do what they were doing." People don't change their behaviors to become more efficient and effective. This is where having a coach or counselor becomes helpful. Reading self-help and/or motivational books are very important; however, if you do not truly undertake the suggestions given, it will not help. Just reading will not make the changes in your life. It continuously takes a conscious effort and persistent action to make the necessary changes to improve your life and move on. It is an effort to write down daily steps to do, to review and rewrite any short-term and/or long-term goals, but also to act on them. Your life will not change by saying what you want to do. You need to do what you say you are going to do. So, get off your bottom and get to work. Make your life what you want it to be. Dream your dreams. Live your dreams because in the end, no one can change your life but you. There is no one to blame. You are the one in charge of making your dreams come true. Just believe and ACT. Vision what you want, daily. Make it happen. Live your life as you dream, as if it has already become real.

# CHAPTER TWELVE
# *Where Do You Want to Be?*

*R*emember how I mentioned to you in the first section of this book, how with each loss in your life, be it loss of a job, a divorce, loss of independence, whatever, you will become the person you are meant to be if you only use these experiences to grow from? You really need to think about what you are meant to learn from each experience. What has the person taught you in life? What has the whole situation taught you? You need to figure that out, and learn and grow from it. Everything happens for a reason. It is just looking past the pain to realize what you can learn from it. This isn't always an easy thing to do. When you are in pain it is difficult to say, "Hey, what can I learn from this?" But, you need to. This will help you grow as a person and help you to become who you are meant to be. This is not something you do right after your loss, in this case, the loss of your sibling. This is after you have accepted the loss and you can think more clearly to learn from the situation. If you have accepted the loss, but are still in immense pain, this is where it is helpful to push yourself to ask yourself this important question. If you cannot heal from it, don't expect to do any growing yet. First, cope with the loss, accept it, and heal. When you are in your healing phase, you can then start thinking about what this person has taught you and how you can grow from this.

What I did was think of things Gary always said to me. One of those was he did not worry about me because he knew I would always be able to take care of myself. This also passed on to my parents after he died. My dad would always say he worried about my two other sisters for different reasons; however, he felt bad I had a difficult time being a single mom and worked so hard. However, he never worried about me because Gary always felt so strongly that

I would always take care of myself and make whatever needed to happen…happen. At times, this made me feel bad and I would joke with Gary and my dad, "Thanks, nobody worries about me." Then, I really started to understand what they both meant. I do make things happen. Things always end up being okay or better than okay. This book is proof. I have worked hard, not always successfully, but I do make things happen to take care of my girls and myself. If I fail at something, I pick myself up, learn from it and start all over again. This is one thing I have learned from my brother, I am a strong person. I can and will take care of myself and will make a success of my life. This is probably the most important thing I have learned from my loved ones who have died, from my grandpa to my brother, to my father. All three of them would always tell me I would be okay that I was a strong girl; so, I grew up knowing and feeling this. I did not always feel strong, but deep down I always knew I would make it through whatever it was I was going through. Sometimes we do not have our lessons so readily visible to us. I have learned other things from my brother. He taught me how to fix things. Never be afraid to try to do something. Nothing was ever out of reach, if only I tried. If I messed up, I could always learn how to do it right, but at least I tried. This is something I have carried on since my brother passed away.

You have to think about the things taught by your sibling, even if it may have been a negative, such as, "My brother drank a lot. I do not want to do this." You learned a valuable lesson from your brother, not to drink. Maybe not drinking and driving, or not to speed, etc. These are all valuable lessons to learn from them, if not from their life, but from their death. There is always something to take from their loss. Finding the lesson they are teaching you, makes you more of the person you are meant to be. It may take time, but *YOU WILL* grow from it. Trust in your sibling. Trust in yourself.

Write down everything you can think of they may have taught you purposely and maybe just by happenstance. Think about these items. What have you just ignored and what you have used to grow from? How can you use these lessons to make your life where you want it to be? This isn't an easy task that will happen quickly. This is something you need to think about and work on. You may write and rewrite things. However, if you honestly think about this and learn from it...it can definitely change your life, *IF YOU LET IT.*

If you truly moved on, you should clearly be able to think about this. If you just break down, maybe you haven't moved on quite as well as you thought. Give it time if this is the case. When you are ready, you will know. It may just come to you out of the blue. You may just switch jobs or friends, whatever, and not even realize it is because of something you have learned, and is a life-changing, positive event. Give yourself the time and the credit to realize you can do this.

If you are someone who has lost several siblings, this process will take longer. You need to be more patient with yourself to learn these lessons, and the lessons may be much different from each other. You may learn more from one sibling versus another, but you will learn something from each, whether it's to do something or not to do something with your life. Be open to your gut instincts. They will guide you. This is still difficult for me, but I am getting better. My instincts always seem to be right; it is just listening to them when I need to. Listen to your dreams to help you learn and see where you are in your healing and learning process.

Another area you need to look at is who are *YOU* now without your sibling? This goes along with how you have moved on with your life, with your job and with *YOU*. Who are you? Did you really know who you were before your sibling's death? Do you know who you are now, after their death? This is an area many people have difficulty with, even people who have not lost someone close to them; knowing who they are. Many people are stuck in their "roles" that they lose track of who they really are, or never get to know who they are. If you did not know who you were before your sibling's death, you may find out afterwards. With everything that goes on with the death of your sibling, you go through so many emotions you sometimes; learn things from it and about yourself. You may have known who you were before their death, but after life without them, you may lose sight of who you are. This is a difficult time. Many people lose sight of where they are going and who they are. This is common. The problem lies in if you don't find yourself again and don't find where you were going. Your path may change after their death and *YOU* may change. You probably will change, but the goal here is to find the new or original *YOU* and the path, be it new or old, again. This is all part of the healing process. Many people find a different path to follow as far as careers afterwards. Many go to school or go back to school to get a new education to help others, having to do with the means of their sibling's death. Be it a social worker, counselor, psychologist, doctor, etc. The possibilities are endless. I have turned my path into a motivational speaker, author, and life coach and grief counselor. When you become passionate about something, you know it is the right path for you. I have become passionate about helping others learn how to cope in a healthy manner from any loss. If I am in a bad mood, when I start with this work, I can go on and on helping people. It makes me feel happy to know I may have helped even one person during my day.

I changed after my brother died in the respect that I changed careers to help others. My career path changed, but my personality and who I was did not. Now, many years later, I have found my passion of whom and what I am. You may know immediately if you want to change your path and you may not. It may take years, as it did for me. I knew I wanted to do something; I just wasn't sure what it was that I was supposed to do until many years later. There is no right and no wrong. Again, this whole process is very individual. Every step and every fork in the road is up to you. We learn more from our mistakes, so don't be afraid of making mistakes. You will learn and grow from them.

# CHAPTER THIRTEEN
# *Stories of Hope and Inspiration About Moving On*

*I* could not write a second and third section to this book and not have stories of hope and inspiration for you. These are now the stories of moving on. My hope is as you read these stories, you will see how people were able to search their hearts and thoughts, and move on with their new lives without their sibling, and finding how to move on with their new identity and place in the family. You will see how as people move on, their thoughts and actions change and they are able to live their own lives.

When you feel you cannot move on, read these stories and put yourself in this same position, which you are. Feel yourself being at that point if you are not already. Feel their feelings and picture yourself moving on, and being at the next level.

For this section, I asked my authors these questions:
1. What changes/steps have you made in your life in order to be able to move on?
2. How long did it take you to be able to get on with your life?
3. What made you decide to move on?

I asked these questions specifically to show you how different situations can be and how different people react differently in all aspects of healing. Some people have specific things and/or timelines they specifically remember and others do not. Most cannot give a specific amount of time it took to be able to get on with their lives. This shows you how different each scenario really is. This shows you that you are not alone. All of us have been to the point where we feel alone and cannot get on with our lives. Then either you get to a point that something clicks or you just seem ready to move on and live. This is where you can learn things about yourself and see what lessons you have learned from your loss.

As far as me moving on, after Gary died, I had to re-evaluate my whole future. I had a plan before he died that I eventually wanted to work with him after college. With him dying my first week of college, I was lost. Thank God, my parents made me go back to school, at least in body, if not in mind and spirit. I had to rethink what I wanted to do and as stated in the first section, a family friend told me I would be good in Occupational Therapy. I went through college, and kept going and going, liking it, but not really finding my purpose now that Gary was gone.

I did my relaxation techniques and realized Gary really was where he wanted to be, and that was with his girlfriend Diane. This helped me to move on with my life and the fact I saw him that one time in the college courtyard, telling me I was going to be okay and he would continue to take care of me. That was the decisive factor to help me move on. It was a conscious effort on my part though. There were times where I would break down, but it was different. I still could live my life and be happy, but I would really have to tell myself he was happy where he was, and he would not want me to be unhappy.

I don't really remember how long it took me to move on with my life. That is why I purposely put this question into my questionnaire for my authors. This was to show you there really is no time limit. Everyone heals differently and some heal quicker than others do. I want to say it was 4 to 6 months before I really accepted his death, and I mean, really accepted it. It was probably 12 to 18 months total until I moved on with my life and really was able to focus on me.

Again, this is a process, a very individual process. There may not be a "moment" that you very well can see when you moved on, and there probably will not be one single thing that happened or didn't happen that made you decide to move on. I think I actually did make a conscious effort to move on because I felt I had to help my parents with things. I was not taking over Gary's life, but I felt I had to take over with doing the things Gary did to help my parents. He did a lot in the yard, fixed cars and boats and everything. That I could not do, but I would carry heavy things so my dad wouldn't have to and would cut the grass or try to help out like he did by helping my dad change the oil in the tractor or winterize and summarize the boat. This was very difficult, however, it made me more into the person I was meant to be. I would not change that for the world. As I have said, my grandfather, father and Gary helped make and mold me into the person I am now. I am very grateful for their passing on their wisdom, insight and knowledge to teach me.

I ask you now to read and feel the strength these survivors are giving you and let go of your pain. I hope that when you read these stories you will recognize yourself in some or all of them.

## *Kelly's Story*

It has taken me a long time to move on with my life. Everyone is different and deals in a different way. For me, at first, it was very hard to get on with my life. I didn't think it was possible. I knew I had to for my daughter, parents and sister. Bret was such a young man who had the world ahead of him. He loved life and lived it to the fullest. Time does help and it has taken a lot of time–years–for me to accept.

I continue to have my sad moments and always will, but I also think of Bret in many situations, knowing he would want our family to be happy, not sad. That keeps me going.

## *Michelle's Story*

The biggest step/change I made was leaving a bad 20-year relationship. I realized what I wanted and knew where I wanted to be, and that was out of the relationship. I reflected on where I was at and where I wanted to be. You are here today and gone tomorrow. Was this where I wanted to be? No, it wasn't! I had to have the tragedy of my brother's life to make a difference in mine. I took his routes and made the necessary changes in my life. I had to think,

"If I went tomorrow, is this where I would want to be?" I knew it wasn't.

I got a divorce, and the kids and I made a new life for us. My brother made his choice and he is in a much better place now. I had to make mine to move on and I am in a much better place now, too.

My brother was missing for a month before we found him. I never really went through a grieving process, I don't believe. I couldn't, I had too much to do. I just kept myself busy with many changes. I did what needed to be done so I really just got on with my life right away; I was so engrossed with finding him. I got through it by finding him and his killer. This is how I found closure in my grieving process.

I played a major role in my brother's case. By fighting to have "Life" at the end of his killer's sentence, it definitely put closure to his loss for me. This helped me to get over it immediately.

The major thing that made me decide to move on was "LIFE!" Life helped me move on. I had my parents; my kids still had to go to school. I still had to go to work. Life had to go on. My brother did not die in vain—I learned from him.

## *Nora's Story*

The Suicide Survivors Group was key for me moving on. I watched others begin to focus on healing and move forward with their life. For me, moving forward entailed simply making a conscious decision that it was time to try to remember what was important to me before and how it had changed, and then to pick a direction and actually start moving. I don't think it really matters what people choose to move forward on, but that they make the choice and then force themselves, at first, to do it.

I needed to move towards life. My husband and I decided to adopt children. We had tried to have birth children for many years and it was not possible. Family was important to me, and family in my mind…entailed children. It is interesting in some ways because we ended up adopting our oldest son whose prognosis was very dire at the time. We were told he would probably die by the time he was five-years-old. It was love at first sight for us, looking at this tiny, little boy who was 4 months old and very frail. Now some people might say, "How could you take a chance like that. Setting yourself up for more loss?" In my mind, I thought about my brother who was physically healthy and yet died. I also thought about a woman I used to work with. She had a beautiful and healthy five-year-old daughter who was killed getting off the school bus when she first began kindergarten. I decided there were no guarantees for any of us and if living entailed risk, then I could either hide under my covers or jump into the void of the unknown with gusto. My son Nicholas was my jump into the void and the future.

Before my brother Steven died, I could hide from the scariness of life, the uncertainty of life by saying to myself, "That will never happen to me." Steven's death shattered that illusion, but in some ways also freed me. If life was a crapshoot, why not take a chance? It dawned on me that any child could die, even stepping off a school bus. You could do everything right and your child could still die. No one could control everything. Recognizing the fact I could not control the future any more than I could have controlled the past was freeing.

I started the suicide survivor group about 1-1/2 years after my brother died and ran the group for 4 years. I wanted someone else to take the keys after the first 2 years, but was not afforded exit because no one from the group would take on the responsibility. As people healed they left the group, but there were always new people coming in with fresh grief, and I couldn't turn my back on them. I feel very strongly people need to be able to enter a group and leave a group when they are ready. It is critical to allow people to move forward and that is very hard to do when one foot is in the future and the other foot is in the past. It was the first group of its kind in our area and there was no one willing or able to run it. Today the group is run by our local Hospice Center.

Please understand it was not that I somehow forgot my brother or was done grieving for him. I simply decided to come to terms with the fact my life was altered, different and it was time to re-group and change direction. I needed a new focus that did not revolve around his suicide. It was 28 years ago that my brother died and I still think of him, miss him and wish he were part of my life.

About the same time I started the group, I also started graduate school. A part of me kept struggling to move forward. To stay in the same place was too painful.

We adopted our oldest son 7 years after my brother died. Nicholas did not die. He is a healthy and happy 21-year-old now, who just graduated from college. We went on to adopt two more sons who are now 19 and 18-years-old. They are great children who are beloved by everyone.

I can't necessarily put a number of years down as to how long it took me to move on with my life. Each little step was a step into the future and a step towards healing. Am I healed totally? I don't think so. Does anyone ever totally heal from this? My goal today is not to totally heal. My goal today is to have a meaningful life.

The painfulness of staying in the same place made me want to move on.

## *Tracey's Story*

After losing my brother, Rick, to suicide in 2004, I was desperate to make sense of how my beautiful, easygoing and seemingly happy brother, who I thought I knew so well, could take his own life. I felt without understanding why he did it, I could not move on or accept what had happened. I needed to understand suicide on a cognitive level too. I had to understand what it feels like to be suicidally depressed and how a suicidal person can disregard the love from their families and friends. How could that not be enough to sustain them? Plagued by a million unanswered questions, I needed answers, and a clearer understanding of suicidal depression. I began to read every book I could get my hands on about suicide. I learned a great deal, about what happens mentally to a person who has lost all hope, feels like a burden to others and who can see no other way to end their immeasurable emotional pain besides suicide. In addition to my reading, I went to a cognitive therapist who helped me understand depression and how it alters a person's perceptions, causing them to see everything as dark and hopeless. Lastly, I also attended a support group. This helped me to feel less alone in my grief.

I don't know if I can say how long it took me to "Move On." It's a long, difficult process with a suicide loss. The loss is complicated by so many unanswered questions, anger, shock and guilt. I can say the first year was riddled with all of the above, especially shock. The second year was absolutely torture. I felt like I was being choked by the guilt and anger took me over, often. I do think after the second year, I began to feel a lightening of the grief. I was able to cope with the loss in a different way. I believe the intensity of the pain changed in the third year. The frequency of the crying bouts also decreased in the third year.

I don't think I made a conscious decision to move on. I think it just happens because grief loosens its grip on you a little at a time. It is similar to a rip tide dragging you down. Once the ocean lets you up a little, you start swimming as fast as you can to get away from it. It may pull you back a little, but it's not as strong and as powerful. I think that after grieving intensely for two years, I was desperately trying to feel "normal" again. It is impossible to be the person I was before I lost my brother, but I am a lot closer to the "old" me than I ever thought possible.

# Part Three
# "Reflections"

## INTRODUCTION

*S*o time has moved on, you have accepted and coped with your sibling's death and have been able to move on with your life (or not). This is where you can really reflect back on your life with and without your sibling. You still will have sad days and even some bad days. This is normal. You are allowed to miss your sibling, to cry to them, for them and want them. Allow yourself this. If you still have issues with living your life without your sibling and cannot live a normal, fulfilling life, you definitely need to seek professional help at this time. I hope that you are living your life and are able to look back, laugh and even cry at those happy times you had with your sibling, and even since your sibling has passed, but know that they would have enjoyed those special times in your live as well.

# CHAPTER FOURTEEN
## *Reflections*

*D*eath is universal. We are not immune from it by age, gender, ethnicity, financial success, etc. The only thing we can control is our reactions to how we cope and deal with death, and how we move on after the death, and learn and grow from them. I hope that after reading this book and getting to the third section, you understand where you are in your coping process and you are able to reflect on how far you have come in your healing. You will experience many losses in your lifetime and with each one, my hope is you will learn and grow with each. It isn't expected for each loss to get easier for you. But maybe, just maybe, it will be easier to see the way to living again; learning you need the time to heal and cope, but that you can learn and grow from each loss, and that you will always carry the memories of your loved one. Nobody can ever take that away from you.

When you are able, reflect back on where you were when your sibling died, and see how far you have come and celebrate that healing. Celebrate your sibling's life, not their death. You are not the same person you were when your sibling was alive. You are a different person leading a different life with different thoughts and beliefs. This doesn't mean you cannot have the same beliefs, actions and thoughts. I am saying that once you go through these changes in your life with the loss of a sibling, you do change. How you react and act to things changes. This doesn't have to be a bad thing. It may even be a great thing. You need to make changes to cope. You may change back to some degree, but maybe not. The main thing here is have you grown as a person? Have you reflected back on your sibling's life, learned something from them and made your life better because of that?

What have you done differently in your life? Where are you right now mentally, physically, in your career, in your spiritual beliefs, etc.? At this point, my hope and goal is that you can reflect back on this time since your sibling died and be able to accept it, and know you still have a life to live and can actually change your life for the better. Yes, I said change your life for the better. Many people, as you have read, have changed their lives and/or careers and grown from the experience. Don't feel guilty looking back on this. Your sibling would be proud you were able to make your life better, as Michelle said in her "Moving On" story, "Do not let your sibling's death be in vain. Learn something from it and make your life better because of it."

While you're reflecting, think of where you truly are right now and where you thought you would be before you ever thought your sibling would be gone. You may have reached your goals you had for yourself, possibly not taking the same path as you had planned, but still reaching your goals. You may have taken a completely different path in your life, one you never would have expected and are working on, or have reached new goals for your new, changed life. Maybe you have not reached goals and may not even have goals. You may feel lost. This is where getting counseling or coaching can help you see where you are and where you want to be, and can help you make decisions and goals for yourself. I moved on with my life in a great direction with good goals and reached those goals, constantly making new ones. However, I always was looking for more. I knew I needed to do something big, something meaningful to help others. I just did not know what *THAT* was. It took me many years of trial and error to find my purpose.

I used my occupational therapy background to assist me in my search. If I had known about life coaching many years ago, I definitely would have searched it out to assist me with my goals. Without outside help, my search took longer, with several years of research for accepting and moving on after a loss. After I decided what I wanted to do, I did get coaching through Jack Canfield's group, which helped me in my coaching and writing immensely.

They taught me by questioning me, how to find what I want and how to get what I want by goal writing.

The whole process is not easy. I will not sugarcoat anything. It is hard work and at times difficult to stay with, and you will have some off days. However, you always have to look at the end result and envision your life as you want it. Envision it as if you already have it. The more you see your life the way you want it, the more real it becomes and the quicker you will reach that life, as long as you stay on your path. You cannot just envision getting over your sibling and having a great life, reaching your goals without doing anything about it. It takes work, but is most definitely worth it.

Here is where the goal writing especially comes into play. If you have been steered away from your goals because of your sibling's death, and found a new life with new goals, that is great, as long as they are putting you where you want to be. However, if your sibling's death has steered you totally away from your goals to nowhere, that is not good. Reflect back on what your goals were before your sibling died. Why can you no longer work toward those goals? Is there a true reason you cannot, such as this is not where you want to go, or is it because you are not motivated yet to do so? If it is a motivational factor, you need to work on that. Find a support group, counseling or a life coach. If you are just feeling lost right now, and don't know which way to turn or what you want to do, you need to write down goals. If this is difficult for you, again, find a coach, friend or someone who can help you. Go on the internet and do those career tests to give you some ideas. Write down your interests, things you have a passion for or things that are fun for you to do and really enjoy. After you have written items down, write down how you could possibly turn that passion into a job. You would be amazed how you can be creative and get a paycheck out of a passion. Try to remember, there is a light at the end of the tunnel. There really is. Many times, it may seem like there is not, but there is. Sometimes you just need to think back of what your goals were before and assess whether these goals still fit your personality and new lifestyle. Your personality and lifestyle very well may have changed after your sibling's death. You may need to re-evaluate your goals and dreams to be who you truly are meant to be.

I want you right now to write down what you remember your goals to be before your sibling died, if appropriate. This will help you to see where you were before and where you are now. Okay, once you have those written down, write down any goals you have now, even if some of the same, or all the same. Have a page that says, "Previous Goals," and one page that says, "Future Goals." Once done writing both down, see where they are similar and where you have made real changes. This is probably because of how you have changed since your sibling's death. Many of our authors for this book, especially the suicide survivors have changed their lives, mostly to the social work fields. They learned from their siblings and wanted to give back, and help others who have gone through the same thing. I know some of their goals were different before their sibling's death.

When a sibling dies, for whatever reason, it changes you. This is why I have asked you to "Reflect" back on where you were to where you are now. Look at how you have changed and/or grown. Looking back on these changes may also help you with your healing and growing process.

# CHAPTER FIFTEEN
# *Reflections on Stories of Hope and Inspiration*

*T*his chapter, showing people's reflections on their stories of hope and inspiration, is here to help you look back on where you were, where and what you have become because of your sibling's death. It will show you how you have changed, if you have, and where you thought your life would be and where in reality, it really is. My hope here is that you now are able to see you were able to learn something from your sibling dying and be able to move forward truly into a life you are meant to be in. One that is positive and fulfilling and maybe even giving back in the same direction your brother/sister died from. This is not to say if your sibling recently passed away, don't expect that when you get to this section, you should be at this point. You will not be, so please don't expect yourself to be. I hope that by now you have learned this is an individual process and it takes time.

The questions I asked for the Reflections sections were:
1. As you reflect back on this time of grieving, accepting, coping and moving on, how have you grown as a person?
2. What were the best things you did that helped you?
3. What things, if any, did you do that did not help, or worsened the situation?

When I reflect back, my goals were I was going to work with Gary, working on heavy equipment. When I was able to look back on those 2 to 3 years after he died, I could not even imagine myself doing that kind of work, even though at the time, I could not imagine doing anything else. It even makes me laugh now to Gary. Doing Occupational Therapy Assisting and killing my back on lifting people all day, I could not imagine sitting on heavy equipment all day and be in the position of having the extensive back pain he was having. My goals definitely changed after his death. When I reassessed my goals, I knew I wanted to be in the health care field to help others who were in accidents and lived. It took many years into my adulthood to really know my purpose, to get into the life coaching, speaking and writing books to help others. This is something I am definitely passionate about. I become a completely positive person when I am doing this work; the type of person I have always strived to be. When I am down or aggravated, I do my work and my disposition completely changes.

## *Kelly's Story*

I do picture what his life would be like now…a young father, with a beautiful wife, a nice home, funny, smart, and full of jokes. I can only make him proud of me. If I ever find myself in negativity, I think of Bret and turn my attitude around.

## *Michelle's Story*

As I reflect back on my time of grieving, accepting, coping and moving on, I see that I have grown tremendously. I enjoy life more. I am more practical and I have become stronger. I was in a bad relationship for 20 years and now I am okay. I savor every moment. I think I have grown a foot! I am more positive now. If I make a mistake in life, I learn from it, so it is no longer a mistake. I learned a lot from the loss of my brother. He did not die in vain!

When I think about what were the best things I did that helped me, I think it would be just making a lot of conscious decisions. I am the backbone of the ones that could not do it alone and being the backbone has always been the positive in the family—picking up the pieces and making everything okay. That helped me a lot. Conscious decisions and changes, I am the post on the fence!

None of the things I did in my healing process made things worse. None of them made it bad!

# Nora's Story

In reflecting back, priorities for me have changed. I try to stop the smell of coffee, so to speak. Enjoy the good moments. I realize everyone has loss and my loss is not unique. It's not the losses we experience, but our ability to persevere through that loss that is important. I don't worry about dying anymore because I realized along the way that it is not how long we live, but what we do with our life that is important. I feel grateful I had my brother in my life for as long as I did. We can't change the past, but the future is still an unwritten book.

The best things I did helped me, without a doubt, the best thing I did was starting the Suicide Survivor Group. Even though it was not a perfect set-up, in that I had to facilitate the group, it still helped a lot. One of the things I announced at every meeting of our group was that I was in the same spot as them and was not the leader simply because I held the keys to the building where we met. This announcement helped somewhat, although the group generally viewed me as the facilitator anyway. I always told them I was there for myself because I struggled with the same issues of loss. I needed to be around others who lost someone to suicide. I had to understand it, grieve with others that "got it." It broke my isolation. I don't know where I would have been without the people who also shared their grief at losing someone they loved to suicide. We found our way together. We found information on other suicide survivor groups and modeled ours after them. I also had a very supportive husband who hung in with me through it all.

For what things, if any, that I did that did not help and/or worsened the situation, was in the very beginning, I wanted my life to be like it was before my brother died. That was futile. I also expected my family to talk about it and heal in the same time frame.

Everyone moves along at the rate they can. I had to accept that even within one's family each person would view it differently at times and grieve it differently as well.

# Desi's Story

I met Desi when I was almost finished with the book and she told me about her story of hope and inspiration. She had lost her sister to complications of diabetes. Later on, she told me how she had also lost her brother in an arson fire.

### Desi's Story...

My sister's name was Jasmine Denise Frazier. We called her "Jazz" for short. Jazz was born on September 5, 1972, and her life ended on April 5, 2006. Jazz died after being in a coma. She was diagnosed as a diabetic early in life at the age of seven-years-old, maybe younger or older, but not much older. She had complications with her diabetes all her life. This last time when she came out of her coma, we the family had to, babysit her, feed her and give her her meds. She really wasn't supposed to eat anything by mouth, but did eat pureed food and some other food, and when she didn't want to eat, she was fed by tube. She also had a heart attack while she was in the coma. We dressed her and took her to the bathroom. Jasmine was like you and me before she went into her coma, driving, living on her own, cooking and cleaning. She graduated from Tri-C and became a teacher for kids with autism. She lived that job. She always put GOD first. She had a great attitude with people she knew and didn't know. Most of all, Jasmine loved her nieces and nephews.

When Jasmine died, a huge piece of me died with her. Jasmine was the oldest of six kids. Now that Jazz was gone, it's like I have to step into the role model now. I wasn't ready for that at all. However, I did learn to adjust. She used to buy the kids school clothes, school supplies, book bags and anything else they needed. Now I help as much as I can. She didn't have any kids. I remember calling her for advice and now I call my sister under me for advice. Man, her death changed my life. I am now the big sister. It's hard. I love my sisters and brothers. As I said, this was something I was not ready for.

My coping with her death was not easy and it's still not. I look at some of her pictures in the photo albums I have, like 4-5 albums. I always feel sad when I do look at them and start crying, and then something always puts a smile on my face. I think about all the great times we had together.

My life has a positive attitude now. I don't cry as much. I can actually talk about her without crying, like when people on the street used to ask her for money, no hesitation. She would reach for change and give them a couple quarters. Now I do the same. Even if I don't have any, I still give them change. It could be my angel.

To those that have dealt with a loss of a sibling, do what that person would do in a bad situation. Be the best you can be. It's not easy. You will never get over it. Think about all the good times the family had together. Trust and believe on the holidays, birthdays, graduation, marriages and births of new family members, you will cry. Think good thoughts and soon you won't cry at all. This is how I dealt with my loss.

I never moved on. There's still a piece missing. However, as I said, I smile and laugh at the thought about the good times. I just kept living and since I am the oldest, I have to stay strong. If I break down, they (siblings) would too. We (sisters and brothers) are a lot closer now than ever.

I wish they would find a cure for diabetes and the things she went through. When she was sick, she would ask God to take her home. I just wish she wouldn't have said that, but God has a plan for us all, and he did take her home, way too soon. We were only a year apart. My sister is now gone. I miss her dearly, but I feel like I have to keep moving on. Sometimes I feel like giving up and something keeps on pushing me to stay stronger for me and everyone else.

I can still remember the day she came to me in my dreams. This was at my old house where I was living at the day she died. In my dream, I was sitting on my bed and I was facing the closets. I saw something move and I went to go closer to the closet, and she jumped out and said, "Boo." I couldn't do anything but laugh and say, "You thought you scared me Jazz!" When she came out, I saw the prettiest big blue sky and wings attached to her shoulders. We talked for a while and she said she was okay, and I have nothing to worry or be scared about. Ever since then, I smile and think about that. I still cry, but not as often. She does come to me every now and then. She is truly my inspiration and others', as well.

~~~~~~

Shortly after Desi gave me her story, she mentioned to me that her brother also died in a house fire. She said the fire was arson. He died on July 4, 2009. She stated it is so hard with one loss, but even more difficult with multiple losses. She uses her faith to help her through it and it helps her to get stronger every day.

Desi also stated the person who set the fire turned herself in to the police 3 days after the fire, and is in jail for a long time! She said it took her longer to get over her brother, being her second sibling, and because it was so different. She said it was harder because it was murder from arson. It was hard enough with diabetes, but this was murder.

## *Laura's Story*

Here we go again! Another year and another Labor Day weekend, it is September 2010 and 29 years since the tragic and unexpected death of our brother at the age of 28. His life was cut far too short, but that night also gave us excitement. There was great news that our sister was expecting. It makes you wonder how there can be tragedy and joy all within a matter of hours.   Personally, to me, I still struggle with our brothers' death. You keep asking, "Why," but the question is always unanswered. You just take it one day at a time. At times, you feel he is better off. He doesn't have to deal with all the trial and tribulations that occur in our everyday lives.

This November will be a year since the unexpected death of our father. I can barely get over my brother, now it's trying to deal with the loss of dad. I am working on the healing process, however slow it may be, but we have our families. One last thing, love and miss you, Gary and dad. Keep watching over all of us and we will reunite again!

## Jeanette's Story

My brother has been gone close to 3 decades now…more years than we had together as siblings. My memories are like little vignettes now; times we spent boating, family trips, bowling and squabbles over TV stations, to name a few. Since his passing, I have experienced countless losses of those who died too young by car accidents, cancer and other illnesses, suicides, drowning and freak accidents—friends, acquaintances and community members who have lost their children. Now, as a parent, this is the worst loss I can ever imagine and pray I never have to experience. I think back on my parents and the unimaginable pain they incurred. Now, it seems somehow less tragic as a sibling, but in reality, any loss of a loved one is tragic, sad, painful, lonely, and all those other feelings we all have when someone we loves leaves us.

I remember the feeling of being in a horrible dream. That I would wake up and everything would be okay. The feelings of disbelief and shock were so strong. I missed a week of work when my brother died. As sad as I was, I had responsibilities and as they say, "Life goes on." I was pregnant with my first child at the time of my loss and it was incredibly important for my health and the health of my baby to take care of myself both mentally and physically. I had that distraction along with my job.

Life is full of disappointments, sadness and happiness, grief, reflection, birth and death, and unless you can face and accept, you can't move forward. I chose to move forward. I mourned the loss of my brother and was sad for the empty spot it left in my heart and in our family, but I forged ahead by surrounding myself with my family and friends, and allowing myself to enjoy in my interests, activities and those I love.

Granted, accepting death has never been easy for me. Many, many tears have fallen, but I have always been a person who outwardly expresses my feelings. I don't hold much inside! I think that is what contributes to my ability to move forward. My parents never sheltered us from knowing or experiencing loss. From a young age, I attended funerals of deceased family members, relatives and friends. I knew bad/sad things happen and I learned to work through them—not always understanding why they happened. As I grew older and became more connected spiritually, I put these events in God's hands and I was able to move on by knowing God had a plan. I trusted Him.

Above all, I have let myself grieve. I have given myself permission to cry when I am sad or when I feel powerless. I know it is okay to feel despair and to find happiness in all that we are given in life, even when it is taken away all too soon.

# *In Closing*

Congratulate yourself on finishing this book. I hope that after reading this you have realized you are not alone in this loss and even though you may feel like you will never get over your loss, you can see that others, who thought the same thing, including myself, actually moved on and made themselves a happy life. It may be a new life, a different life, but it is your life. You can live a happy, productive life, just like the authors and me, as written here. If you still have not accepted your sibling's loss and it has been a year or two, I suggest you talk to a professional. You don't need to suffer and not live. Give yourself the permission to move forward and live your life to the fullest.

My hope is that you have gotten some hope and insight from this book to see life can and will go on. I hope that you will be able to move on with not just your personal life, but also your career, and are now better able to understand yourself, as a person and realize who you are and what you want in life.

Remember whatever life you want is your choice. You can continue to be upset and not live, or you can lift yourself up and deal with your loss, learn something from it and move on. This is showing respect to your sibling, not stopping your life. Move on in honor of them. Do something positive for yourself, your life. Grow from this experience. Do not feel guilty for living and being happy. Things happen for a reason. We may never know the reasons, but God has his plan for us all. We do not have control over death, but we do have control over how we react and act to death, and what happens in our lives. We have the choice to be proactive and positive; to learn and grow and accept the situation, versus being passive and ignoring the situation, hoping it will go away by doing nothing, while we die day by day, not living our one precious life. Reflect on this…Move On…Be inspired.

A moment of reflection back on our siblings and gratefulness for them being in our lives, not nearly long enough, but yet enough to enlighten our lives. Let us be grateful to them and for them.

# *Acknowledgements*

Mom and Dad, there are no words to thank you for all you have done for me. Your love and respect have meant the world to me. You have always encouraged me to be my best and go for my dreams. It took me a while, but you never said not to try anything. Thank you for your insight and guidance, and especially your love.

Chris, if it were not for you, this never would have come to fruition. Your encouragement and love helped to get me back on the path to completion, even after all the obstacles put in my life. Thank you for keeping me focused and on the right path, and hanging in there with me through it all.

Andrea and AnaMaria, thank you for listening to all my stories when you were bored to death and sick of hearing about "the book." I love you both dearly and thank you for all your support and help throughout this endeavor.

To Cathy Simone and Charlie Knudson, how can I thank you? Cathy, you have been my mentor and sounding board throughout all of this. I never would have known where to begin without your support and knowledge. Continued luck to you with your IC books and your future endeavors.

To all my authors, who open-heartedly contributed their stories to help others. Without all of you, this book would not offer the insight it does. I thank you all. To my editors, Laura Kasner-Blake, Kelly Scanlon-Pitman and Jimmy Shaarda for their hours and hours of reading and editing all my commas out. I thank you all from the bottom of my heart.

To all family and friends, who have listened to all my "book" stories and waiting to see if it would finally be finished. Thank you for your patience with my stories and talking.

# BIBLIOGRAPHY

All About Prayer (2009). In *Power of Prayer – Supernatural.* Retrieved 03/28/09, from http://www.allaboutprayer.org/power-of-prayer.html
Counselingstlouis.net
Finley, Guy (2009). Touch the Timeless Truth of Yourself. In *Life of Learning Foundation.* Retrieved 06/07/09, from http://www.guyfinley.com/key_Lessons/Expanded_Lessons/Further_Understanding/3642/?...
Griefworks BC, a Partnership between Children's & Women's Health Centre of British Columbia and Canuck Place Children's Hospice. *Death of a Brother or Sister.* Retrieved 03/18/09, from http://www.griefworksbc.com/SiblingDeath.asp
The Highly Sensitive Person Survival Guide (2009). In *Coping Strategies.* Retrieved 03/07/09, from http://www.hspsurvival.com/_coping.html
Kessler, David (2009). *The Five Stages of Grief – Elisabeth Kubler-Ross and David Kessler.* Retrieved 03/08/09, from http://grief.com/the-five-stages-of-grief/
Legacy Connect (2009). Harper Neeld, Elizabeth, Ph.D. In *Do Men Grieve Differently from Women?* Retrieved 05/15/09, from http://www.connect.legacy.com/inspire/page/show?id=1954035%3APage%3A2170.
The Light Beyond: You are not alone in your grief (2009). In *10 strategies for coping with grief.* Retrieved 03/07/09, from http://www.thelightbeyond.com/10_strategies_for_coping_with_grief.html
The Light Beyond: You are not alone in your grief (2009). In *When a Sibling Dies.* Retrieved 03/07/09, from http://www.thelightbeyond.com/death_of_a_sibling.html
 MacArthur, Catherine and John D (2009). Research Network on Socioeconomic Status and Health. In *Coping Strategies.*

Retrieved 03/07/09, from http://www.macses.ucsf.edu/Research/Psychosocial/notebook/Coping.html

Marrone, Robert. *Death, Mourning & Caring.* Thomson Wadsworth. 2007.

Meyer, Robert G. & Weaver, Christopher M. *The Clinician's Handbook. Integrated Diagnostics, Assessment, and Intervention in Adult and Adolescent Psychopathology.* Fifth Edition. Waveland Press, Inc. 2007.

Opentohope.com

Paul Chek from SelfGrowth.com

Spirit Home (2009). In *Power of Prayer – Supernatural.* Retrieved 03/28/09, from http://www.spirithome.com/faith-sp.html

Walsh-Burke, Katherine. *Grief and Loss: Theories and Skills for Helping Professionals.* Pearson Education, Inc. 2006.

Welshons, John E. and Dr. Wayne Dyer. *Awakening From Grief (Finding the Way Back to Joy).* Inner Ocean Publishing, Inc. 2003 by John E. Welshons.

# WORKBOOK

## *Journal Notes*

Journaling is a good way to clear your thoughts and help you heal. Try getting into a habit of journaling daily. It doesn't have to be anything fancy, just write to help you release your thoughts. I advise getting a notebook/journal for your daily/weekly entries.

_____

_____

_____

_____

_____

_____

_____

_____

_____

_____

_____

*Coping with the Loss of a Sibling: I Miss You, Gary*

*Workbook*

*Coping with the Loss of a Sibling: I Miss You, Gary*

# What Have You Been Thinking About so Far Today?

Look at everything you wrote down. Have the things you been thinking about today been mostly negative or positive? Go through each item and next to it write down "positive" or "negative" to correspond with the thought.

Do you feel you need to put closure to your sibling's death? Write down what things you can think of to help you put closure to your loss. It may be things like cleaning up some of their things, going to see their gravesite or going to see a significant other. Anything that comes to your mind, write down.

_____
_____
_____
_____
_____
_____
_____
_____
_____
_____
_____
_____

# Goal Writing

Have you ever written goals down before? You probably thought them to yourself, but maybe never actually wrote them down. I would like you to write them down because it makes you more accountable to work towards reaching them.

First, there are short-term goals. These small steps help you attain your main goal, what you eventually want to do, or become, etc.

Think of your long-term goal. Now, what small steps or goals can help you reach this long-term goal? For an example, say your long-term goal has nothing to do with your sibling, but has to do with buying a house. You feel it will be a new start to a new life. What small steps can you take to help you buy this house? Maybe one is you need a better job. So there is one short-term goal, it can be as small as researching other opportunities and making three calls per day about a new job.

With these short-term and long-term goals, you want to make a deadline for yourself, so you push yourself to work towards it. For example, I will make three calls per day about researched job opportunities for one week. By 05/10/10, at 2 p.m., I will have a job interview set up.

Another short-term goal could be, I will have my house ready to sell by 05/28/10, at 11 a.m. Are you getting the idea? Or, my house will be sold by 06/05/10, at my asking price.

A long-term goal could be, I will buy my dream home to start my new life by 10/10/13, at 4 p.m.

## Short-Term Goals:

_____

_____

_____

_____

_____

_____

_____

_____

_____

_____

_____

_____

_____

_____

_____

_____

## Long-Term Goals:

Along with the short-term and long-term goals, as stated above, you can go one-step further. Each day, either before you go to bed or in the morning, write down 3 things you are going to do that day (or the next day) to help you attain your goals. This can be as simple as making two calls a day, writing and/or typing up your resume, buying clothing needed for an interview, etc.

**Write down the 3 things you are committing to today to do.**

_____

_____

_____

_____

_____

_____

_____

_____

_____

_____

_____

_____

## Quiet Time

Put yourself into a quiet room. Get yourself comfortable and relaxed. You can light a candle and put on some soothing music. Make sure you have a pen/pencil and paper. Write down anything and everything that comes to your mind, even if it doesn't seem like it means anything or sounds like it is something you can work on. Don't look deep into any thought. Just write down every thought you have.

_____

_____

_____

_____

_____

_____

_____

_____

_____

_____

_____

_____

## 50 to 100 Things You Want to Achieve Before You Die (Your "Bucket List")

When I first heard of this activity, I thought there was no way I was going to be able to find that many things I wanted to do before I die. Well, just start and you will see there probably is. It can be, wanting to meet George Clooney, the President, going to Aruba, getting straight A's, etc. Absolutely anything that you want to do, no matter how silly it sounds. This is fun, go do it and enjoy yourself!

_____

_____

_____

_____

_____

_____

_____

_____

_____

_____

_____

_____

*Workbook*

*Coping with the Loss of a Sibling: I Miss You, Gary*

## Vision Board

Another fun activity is to make a vision board. This can be anything you want to achieve or remember on a poster board. It can be pictures of you and your sibling laughing. A vacation site you want to visit or of people laughing. You can print things out from the computer, take pictures of you in the car you want to buy or of exercise equipment; you would like to get to help you heal, etc. Just let your imagination go with this one.

When you are done with this activity, make sure you put it somewhere where clearly visible to you.

Along with this, you could also make a smaller collage of pictures of you and your sibling, pictures that make you happy and remember the good times. Then, when you are sad and having a bad day, look at this collage of happy memories and just *BE* happy.

Look at these vision boards daily. Before you know it, you will see some of your hopes and dreams come alive.

## Gratefulness

Being grateful for what you have and for experiences you have had in your life is a very powerful tool. Once you can truly be grateful for your experiences, you will notice more coming back to you.

Start your day off by saying what you are grateful for every morning when you wake up. Whenever something happens, good or bad, ask yourself what you learned or what you can learn. This can help make your day more positive and fulfilling.

List what you are grateful for at this moment.

_____

_____

_____

*Coping with the Loss of a Sibling: I Miss You, Gary*

*Workbook*

## What Will Help You Heal?

Sit in a quiet room with a pad of paper and pen/pencil. Give yourself 15 minutes to write down anything that comes to mind that may help you heal. Again, don't worry about if it sounds funny. No one needs to see your list. Just write. Then, you can go through each item and see what might really help.

_____

_____

_____

_____

_____

_____

_____

_____

_____

_____

_____

_____

_____

_____

## What Are You Focusing On?

Anthony Robbins asks, in his lecture series, "What are you focusing on this very minute?" Think about this. I want you to write down what you are focusing on right now. Be real honest with yourself.

_____
_____
_____
_____
_____
_____
_____
_____
_____
_____
_____
_____
_____

*Workbook*

Now really look at what you just wrote down. Again, be honest; think about what you wrote down. Is what you wrote truly what you want to be? Remember, WHAT YOU FOCUS ON, YOU BELIEVE. If what you wrote down is not what you want to believe in, then focus on the positives and start moving on.

Look at any negatives you wrote and think about how you can turn them into a positive thought. Do you feel you need to put closure to your sibling's death? Write down things you think would help you to put closure to your loss. It may be things like, cleaning up some of their things, going to see their gravesite or maybe going to see a significant other.

Anything that comes to mind write it down.

*Workbook*

## What does "Moving On" mean to you?

*Workbook*

What things can you do to help yourself reach this goal?

_____

_____

_____

_____

_____

_____

_____

_____

_____

_____

_____

_____

_____

_____

_____

_____

Write down 3 to 5 daily action steps to do each day to keep yourself accountable in reaching your goals.

*Workbook*

What have you already done to move on?

_____
_____
_____
_____
_____
_____
_____
_____
_____
_____
_____
_____
_____
_____
_____
_____
_____

What has helped?

What are you doing or feeling that is holding you back?

Do you feel guilty about moving on? _____ Why?

What positive things have you learned from your sibling's death?

_____
_____
_____
_____
_____
_____
_____
_____
_____
_____
_____
_____
_____
_____
_____
_____
_____

When you reflect back on your time now without your sibling, how are you different?

How have your grown as a person?

_____
_____
_____
_____
_____
_____
_____
_____
_____
_____
_____
_____
_____
_____
_____

Read an inspirational book!

## About the Author

Roberta Costantino has worked in the healthcare field for 25 years, is a grief counselor and life coach, specializing in coping issues. She performs keynote speeches, seminars, workshops and individual or group coaching, to help others cope and move forward in a positive direction to modify their lives.

LaVergne, TN USA
29 March 2011
222067LV00005B/152/P